THE INCOMPLETE GUIDE
TO BUYING AND
SELLING YOUR HOME

THE INCOMPLETE GUIDE
TO BUYING AND
SELLING YOUR HOME

Mark Griswold

Bitterroot Mountain
Publishing House

THE *IN*COMPLETE GUIDE TO BUYING AND SELLING YOUR HOME
Copyright © 2024 Mark Griswold
Published by Bitterroot Mountain Publishing House
P.O. Box 3508, Hayden, ID 83835
www.BMPHMedia.com
Second Edition: 2025

Front and back covers and interior design by Mark Griswold.

Interior illustrations by Glasbergen Cartoon Service.

ISBN 978-1-940025-60-5 Print book

ISBN 978-1-940025-61-2 Ebook

Library of Congress Control Number: 2022900500

Printed in the United States of America

1. Residential Real Estate 2. House Selling 3. House Buying

DISCLAIMER

While every effort has been made to ensure the accuracy of content in this book, laws and accepted practices related to real estate, mortgage, housing, and the environment are constantly changing, and can vary from state to state or even city to city. Some statistics cited in this book may also have changed. Unless otherwise noted, statistics are from the National Association of Realtors.

Because the author conducts most of his practice in Northern Idaho, this book is tailored to the laws of this state. Also included are some references to laws and scenarios in Washington, since he is also licensed and practices there.

Please consult with a licensed real estate agent or other licensed professional before undertaking any real estate transaction or other actions that are covered by the content in this book.

ACKNOWLEDGEMENTS

Thank you to all those who have mentored me throughout my real estate career, but especially the late Wendy Lister, who saw something in me the first time we met and took a chance by hiring me to be part of her team.

Thank you to all my clients. Without you, I would be a real estate agent in name only.

Thank you to my editor, Suzanne Holland, and to Larry Telles and all the other folks at Bitterroot Mountain Publishing House, for helping to make this book a reality.

Finally, and most of all, thank you to my wife, Rosie, who supported me in every sense of the word when I chose to jump off a cliff without a parachute and go into business for myself.

TABLE OF CONTENTS

INTRODUCTION

Welcome to the home buying and selling process. For most of you, buying or selling a home will be a generally positive experience. You are either buying your first home, a truly historic (in a personal sense) and exciting experience; or you are moving into another home for a generally positive reason. To you, I offer my congratulations! You've worked hard to get where you are. This is truly a time to celebrate the opportunity to participate in the American Dream of homeownership, then get to work finding your new home!

Of course, for some of you, buying or selling a home may not be something you are looking forward to doing. Perhaps the sale of your home is due to death, divorce, or financial difficulties. Maybe you've reached a stage in your lives where your current home, as much as you love it, is no longer a practical reality for your lifestyle. Perhaps you are having to move to a new city and are quite nervous about the whole process. To you, I offer my sympathy.

Even in the best of times, selling a home can be almost as painful as losing a family member if those walls contain years of sweet memories. Selling while dealing with everything else a difficult situation poses is just one more thing on an overwhelming list.

To buyers and sellers of all types, I offer this guide as a resource to help smooth the path toward a successful purchase or sale. Regardless of your circumstances, buying or selling a home is a big undertaking for most people and is done infrequently enough that it can be confusing even when all goes fairly well without any surprises.

Speaking of surprises, even for a seasoned real estate agent, something will typically pop up during a transaction that isn't business as usual. In real estate, there is really no such thing as business as usual. Every transaction involves a truly unique home and truly unique people. Thankfully, when both buyers and sellers have good intentions and are working with knowledgeable real estate agents and those who support them (mortgage lenders, title and escrow agents, inspectors, etc.), the two sides in a transaction usually come together in a win-win situation and everyone is happy.

It does take knowledgeable professionals to make this happen, though. Because there are so many moving pieces to buying or selling a home, no one can anticipate everything that may happen. That's why I've titled this book "The *In*complete Guide to Buying & Selling a Home."

I'd love to say it's the *Complete* Guide. Everyone could read a copy and no surprises would come up during the transaction. But it's not complete. In fact, it only skims the surface. Not only is it impossible to anticipate everything that might arise during a transaction that hasn't happened yet, I haven't even included everything that has happened during transactions that I've been involved in. If I did, this book would be twice as long, and your eyes would probably glaze over. Honestly, for some of us who work in real estate, this might be a fascinating read, but I'm guessing you just want to get through the process of buying or selling a home so you can pick out curtains, fire up the grill, and have a great housewarming party with your friends!

So, here's the short version if you don't want to read any further. Hire an experienced and knowledgeable real estate agent. While the investment may seem large at first glance, unless you sell homes on a regular basis, the benefits will almost always far outweigh the cost. There are simply too many things that can come up during a transaction that can't be specifically anticipated. There are also changes to real estate law that happen every year and, if not followed, have the potential to land you in legal trouble.

Selling a home can also be an emotional experience. It pays to have an objective set of eyes to help guide you. But more on all of this and more in the pages to follow, so read on!

For those of you who do read on, after you have, you should know just enough to be dangerous about a lot of things. Hopefully, even if you choose to buy or sell a home on your own, you'll actually know more than just enough to be dangerous, and the tips and tools you'll learn may help you avoid some of the common pitfalls found in a real estate transaction.

I wish you the best of luck in your transactions and you're always welcome to call or email me with questions. I will do my best to answer them.

Mark Griswold
www.refugepropertiesnorthidaho.com

CHAPTER 1
DECIDING TO BUY
OR SELL A HOME

Whether to buy or sell a home may seem like an obvious question to anyone who's picked up this book, but it's worth asking. Buying or selling a home is a big undertaking and it costs money regardless of which side of the transaction you're on. (Sellers may have to pay taxes, listing fees, and costs associated with getting the home physically ready to sell. Buyers have closing costs, including inspection, appraisal, title, and loan fees in addition to the obvious sale price of the home.)

The first question to ask is about your motivation. For sellers, maybe you have to move to a new area, and it seems obvious that you'll have to sell. But do you? It could be more beneficial to rent out your first home, if it covers the mortgage as well as puts extra money in your pocket.

Maybe you need more space. But do you? Maybe you just need less stuff. We seem to be a culture that values "more, bigger, faster," but there does seem to be a trend recently toward "less, smaller, slower." You might be able to solve your *problems* just by getting rid of some of that *stuff* you haven't touched in years. Or maybe you really do need more space but remodeling or adding on to your home would be a better solution.

Maybe you need less space, or the upkeep has become overwhelming. Again, perhaps remodeling and creating a separate space you could rent out could be a solution. Or maybe hiring a cleaning service or a gardener to come regularly, while it might seem like an extravagance, would end up being more economical in the long run.

It could be that you've just grown tired of your home and want something newer. In this case, remodeling, or even just slapping on a new coat of paint and getting some new furniture might be the answer.

For buyers, many of these same questions apply. For first-time buyers, the choice is between continuing to rent or buying something of your own. Real estate is an investment in many ways, not just financially. Over time, the market has always gone up, so, for most people, buying is almost always preferable to renting, but it is a commitment. You will need to take care of your new home and you'll have the financial commitment of a mortgage. (Mortgage comes from the Latin for death pledge, if that gives you some idea of how serious it is.)

For buyers, in addition to deciding whether buying a home is right for you, you'll also need to decide just what type of home you want to buy. Thinking about "less, smaller, and slower," what do you truly need? Are you looking at 6000-square-foot mansions because you really need that amount of space or because you're just in love with something that big? Once you buy it, will you have half that home sitting unused 90% of the time? Think, too, about location. You might have to go some distance out to get the type of property you want, but is it really what you need? Will the extended commute time be worth the extra space? Maybe so, but consider what your time is worth and think about how much happier you might be in the long run with less space, but also less time behind a steering wheel.

WHEN TO BUY OR SELL

If you do decide you want to buy or sell, then the next question is about timing. What is the market doing both seasonally and cyclically? Spring tends to be the best time to sell a home. The weather is better so more people feel like driving around. There's also more sunlight so your home will show better. Buyers with children often start looking in spring. That way, they can complete the purchase in summer and be moved in time for the kids to start a new school in fall.

For buyers, you might want to look in the fall or winter when fewer people are competing for a home. There's more chance that anyone selling their home is more motivated to do so.

Cyclicality refers to overall market trends. Does it favor buyers or sellers? A balanced market has about two months of inventory. In other words, if no more houses were listed, it would take two months for all the houses to be sold. (There are markets within markets, as well. Condos may sell at a different rate than 2000-square-foot ranchers which may sell at a different rate than 10,000-square-foot mansions.) Economists will often predict what the market will look like a few months to a year in the future, but they often get it wrong for a variety of reasons, usually things not happening that they anticipated would (lowering or raising of interest rates, mass migration from one area to another due to changes in the job market, etc.). Even though many of the experts' predictions are often off, it's still a good idea to follow the trends in your community since the market *will* change at some point.

In general, though, real estate always goes up in price over time. Even when the housing market takes a drastic hit like it did in 2008, those who bought right before the crash still regained their equity and then some before too long.

In short, whether to buy or sell a home and when is the first big decision you'll make. Think about the alternatives and consult with a real estate agent before making the final decision.

Just a brief note on touring homes; don't overextend yourself. Try to limit yourself to looking at no more than five homes in a day. More than that, and they will all start to blur together, and you'll forget which features went with which home. Be sure to take notes and pictures of your tour as well. Another good strategy is to compare homes as you go. Ask yourself, "If I had to buy a home right now, and my only options were home one and home two, which one would I pick?" As you view more and more homes, you'll get a better idea of what is really a *need* and what is more of a *want*.

CHAPTER 2
GETTING YOUR HOME
PHYSICALLY READY TO SELL

When you hire a real estate agent, you are ultimately the boss. You're counting on your agent for their expert opinion, but at the end of the day, it's just that, an opinion. Regarding the overall market, no one can predict the future and some event, good or bad, may impact how much your home ends up selling for. Regarding certain decisions about your home, no one can predict an individual buyer's preferences. Should you go with the carpet or the luxury vinyl plank (LVP) when replacing a floor? Maybe it's best not to replace the floor at all and offer a credit to the buyer. There's no definitive answer since not every buyer will want the same thing. That means the final decisions are yours to make.

A good agent should lay out the options in a particular scenario, then tell you what they think the trade-offs for choosing a particular option are. Don't worry about questioning our opinions, either. We're all human and can make mistakes. Maybe you've even thought of something your agent hasn't!

***

So, now you've decided you definitely want to sell your home, and now is the right time. Before you stick a For Sale sign in the front yard, you need to get the home ready to impress buyers. This is, in many ways, the most important part of the process. Your home will sell for more if it looks better with fewer flaws. Physically, your home should be free of chipping paint and worn carpet, for example.

Paperwork-wise, you need to be aware of things such as liens, encroachments, or other surprise encumbrances on your property that you might not even know exist. Some things may have to be resolved in order to sell your home, period.

Of course, it might not be more cost-effective to do some repairs or upgrades, if the cost is going to be more than the likely price improvement will yield. But in many cases, minor and inexpensive things can be done to make your home more attractive to potential buyers. The more potential buyers you have, even to the point where you get multiple offers, the higher the price you're likely to get.

Case in point: we bought our current home in one of the hottest sellers' markets in the country. Average days on the market were less than a week, and most homes received multiple offers on the first day they were listed. This was not the case with the home we bought. It sat on the market for two months, even though it was located in one of the most sought-after neighborhoods in our area. There was nothing significantly wrong with it. It wasn't a fixer-upper, had no issues with the title, and it wasn't even over-priced. (Of course, price does fix everything, just ask those little towns in Italy or the Midwestern United States that will pay you to move there.)

So, what was the problem? The house just didn't *show* well. The owner was present during our viewing, and I'm guessing she was there for other ones as well. Maybe she had her reasons, but when an owner is in a home, buyers tend to spend less time in it.

It also didn't feel clean. It wasn't a hoarder home by any means, and it was clean enough, but it looked lived in. The furniture was also terribly dated. This might not make a lot of sense. After all, we weren't buying the furniture or the rather minimal clutter around the home, but when most people walk into a home, they want to envision it as *their* home. The more it's depersonalized the easier it is for buyers to do so.

People also value space, and the fewer items that are in the home, the bigger it will look. Kitchen counter space is usually an important thing. Even if the new owner is going to put a mixer, a toaster, a bread maker, a crock pot, a dish rack, and a big bottle of dish soap on that counter once they move in, if all that stuff is there when they first look at the home, they may have a tough time envisioning all *their* stuff on the counter.

What I just described is generally referred to as staging or, in the case of the home we bought, a lack thereof. Had the owner painted the walls; put away as many items as possible, including a few pieces of furniture; hired professional cleaners to come in and make every surface sparkle, I have little doubt her home would have sold for the price she was asking within a week of her listing it.

Maybe the owner was too overwhelmed by other things to take the time to address those items, and that's fine. We all make trade-offs of time and money, and they may have been worth it to her. The point is, know the trade-offs you're making. Know what investments of time and money will net you. Typically, many things can be done for relatively little time and money and will earn big gains when the home sells. I'll cover staging in more detail in a bit, but before you get to staging a home, you should make sure it's in its best shape overall. That means repairs.

PRE-INSPECTION

You're probably aware of some of the repairs that need to be done in your home. Some of them you've probably lived with since you bought the home because they're really not an inconvenience. Maybe you've even grown to appreciate the quirks. (Remember the loose newel post that George Bailey loved at the end of *It's a Wonderful Life?*) That's fine for you, and honestly, it's probably fine for your buyers. If someone loves everything about your home except for that one kitchen drawer that requires a little jiggling to get out, they're not going to walk away over it. But do you really want them wondering if that drawer is a symptom of a potentially bigger problem?

I prefer to turn over a home that's in its best condition (within reason). Moving is stressful, and I don't want to start making a bunch of repairs the second I move into a new home (unless I bought it as a fixer-upper).

This is all within reason and no one will walk away over a minor defect, but if it's an easy fix, I believe in making it since the time, skill, and monetary cost invested is usually minimal and will gain big returns. The new owners will greatly appreciate not having to fix anything the moment they move in, and it's just a nice thing to do.

Once you've silenced all the squeaky hinges and filled all the cracks you know about, you should consider finding the problems you don't know about. When was the last time you went into the attic or crawl space? Is that electrical panel (installed in 1972) that has worked perfectly, really nothing to worry about? What about your furnace? Your home is warm enough, so that's nothing to worry about either, right? Maybe. You don't really know until you get a licensed home inspector to take a look.

A licensed home inspection for most homes costs around $600, but it's well worth the investment. I've had sellers assure me their home is fine only to have a fairly major issue come up during the buyers' inspection. Even if the inspector doesn't find anything wrong with your home, you'll have the peace of mind that your home is flawless. In addition, your buyers will have confidence in the home they're buying. Of course, I always encourage buyers to get their own inspections since the inspector will then be liable to them if something comes up after they move in.

In a strong sellers' market, with multiple offers being the rule, and no time to conduct a buyers' pre-inspection, having one done by the sellers can offer at least some assurance of a home that's in good working order.

Another reason to have your home pre-inspected before listing is that you get to choose the inspector. While many inspectors are certified by an organization like the American Society of Home Inspectors (ASHI), and many are good at what they do, there are some who don't know what they are doing or may even be unethical. I listed a house once that I knew to be in good condition, so the seller and I decided to forgo the pre-inspection. The buyers did an inspection, and their inspector claimed the roof had less than five years of usable life on it. The home was only 15 years old and had been built with a 50-year roof that had been well taken care of. In this case, the inspector either had no business being in his profession or was just downright unethical and wanting to create a job for himself.

The deal ended up closing, but the seller did have to come down slightly on the price because I advised him that a home that goes back on the market after it fails an inspection will almost always sell for less, even if the reason for the failed inspection was erroneous.

COMMON ISSUES FOUND IN HOME INSPECTIONS

Plumbing and wiring are often big concerns. If your home is older, it may not be that expensive to address the issue, but you'll definitely want to know about it. For example, homes built before the mid-1970s may have a Zinsco electrical panel. Many of these panels still work today and have never caused an issue. But they have been known to cause fires and some loan underwriters won't approve a loan on a home with a Zinsco panel. This is not something you want to find out about a week before closing, especially when a new panel only takes a few hours to install and typically costs less than $2000, a small price to pay to ensure your home sale goes through.

Foundation issues are typically deal killers if they're major. You may have to spend a lot of money to have them repaired. It's better to know about it beforehand though. The good news is they may not cost much to repair or may not be a significant but may *appear* to be a big issue.

I had a sale almost go sideways once because of a large foundation crack. It looked scary, but it actually didn't affect the structure at all. Because the seller had hired the same inspector he'd hired when he'd first bought the home, the inspector knew the crack wasn't a foundational issue and didn't include it in his report (although he really should have). When the new buyers had the home inspected, their inspector wasn't as well-trained and started making wild claims about it costing $50,000 to repair. This was something outside the scope of his job, which even the buyers' agent agreed he had no business commenting on. While the deal closed, it was stressful for everyone involved, stress that could have been avoided had the inspector mentioned the crack in his report.

Mold can be a red flag, but it's typically far less scary than most people think. Most molds, while they should certainly be cleaned up and the cause addressed, are typically fairly harmless. You'll have some folks, though, even some untrained inspectors, look at any mold and tell you it's the dreaded black mold, and that it will kill everyone unless you completely gut the home. The fact is, most mold problems, once the root cause is addressed, can be easily remediated just by applying a little bleach and repainting the affected area.

Crawlspaces and attics should be clean and rodent free. Access to these spaces also needs to be easy. If an inspector can't get into them, they just won't be included in the report. No news, in this case, isn't good news and you, the seller, may have to pay for a re-inspection all because you didn't move the bookcase that was blocking the crawlspace access. Even a small box in front of an access point may hinder an inspector, either because they don't want to be held liable if they break what's in it, or they're just plain lazy.

For all these reasons, when an inspection is being conducted on your home, while you don't need to be present, you should at least be available and let the inspector know they're welcome to call you with any questions or for help locating things like the water main shut off or sewer access.

Appliances should be in working order. Replace the burned-out light bulbs in the oven and the refrigerator. That's one of those repairs that only costs a few bucks and takes a few minutes. If the appliance itself doesn't work, you should consider replacing it. First, if your home is at a price-point where you may accept FHA financing, it's possible the loan won't be approved because of a broken appliance. You definitely don't want to find this out when you're a week away from closing and have to put your home back on the market because your buyers were looking for a way out and you gave it to them.

Also, if an appliance doesn't work, it may raise red flags with the buyers. If the owners aren't taking care of their appliances, what else aren't they taking care of that might not be seen? It's also just the right thing to do. You wouldn't want to move into a home with a busted freezer, so sell the home you'd want to move into (within reason, of course; you don't need to go out and buy the top-of-the-line stainless steel model).

Finally, an often overlooked but vitally important requirement concerns homes requiring working **carbon monoxide and smoke detectors**. These are required on every floor (including the basement) and inside every bedroom/sleeping area (or just outside if a couple of bedrooms share a hallway). They must be installed on or near the ceiling (highest point on a vaulted ceiling). An appraiser may call it out if these are missing. In new construction, smoke detectors must be hard wired.

THE *DOWNSIDES* TO GETTING AN INSPECTION

The obvious downside is that an inspection is an added expense. $600 is $600. If sellers are absolutely sure there is nothing wrong with their home (maybe they've only lived there a year and are meticulous about getting everything serviced and repaired), then they probably don't need to pay for an inspection. Of course, it can't hurt to have a report to show potential buyers.

The other downside to getting a pre-inspection is that the inspector might find something that's going to cost more to repair than the sellers can afford. If they hadn't had a pre-inspection and didn't know about this, they wouldn't have to disclose it. But chances are, the buyers' inspector is going to find it, and even if they don't, do you really want to be the person who turned over a defective home? Not only is it unethical, in my opinion, it could also expose the sellers to legal troubles long after the sale.

I know of someone who received a nasty letter from an attorney who represented buyers who'd bought their home nearly a year earlier. The buyers had an inspection done, and their inspector didn't find the issue they were later complaining about so the complaint didn't go anywhere. But it's still a good cautionary tale about why sellers should protect themselves by always ordering an inspection.

THE FHA CHECKLIST

If your home price qualifies for FHA financing, and you accept buyers with one of these loans, the FHA will require a particular kind of appraisal. Unlike a conventional loan appraisal, which is typically pretty lenient (the bank may not even send someone out if the loan-to-value is low enough), an FHA appraisal is more stringent. The Zinsco panel is one of the things they'll probably call out. I've even heard of some FHA appraisers calling out peeling paint.

So, what do they typically look for? It can change on the capricious whim of the bureaucrats at the Department of Housing and Urban Development or even the individual appraiser sent to inspect your home, but an FHA-licensed inspector should know the latest guidelines. The most common things to look out for are related to health and safety.

- Is water properly draining away from the home?
- Do all bedrooms have proper egress in case of fire?
- In homes built before 1978, is the paint damaged or peeling?
- Do all stairways have handrails?
- Does the heating system work sufficiently?

- Is the roof in good repair? (FHA appraisers will be more stringent on what they consider *good repair* than a typical conventional loan appraiser.)
- Is the foundation in good repair?

If an FHA appraisal does call some things out, it's probably not the end of the sale. Most items can be easily repaired and re-inspected in time for the loan to close, but as a seller, it will definitely be less stressful if everything is addressed before the first appraisal, so no re-inspection is necessary.

LEAD PAINT, ASBESTOS, AND RADON! OH MY!

There are some other issues you should be aware of in your home. These are not things you necessarily need to fix, but they are atypical or dated, so buyers may ask questions about them, and you'll want to know the answer. ("I don't know" is usually not a good answer to most questions buyers have.)

Lead Paint—The federal government banned the sale of lead-based paint in 1978. Most homes built after that year won't have it. Only the sale of lead-based paint was banned though, so if a builder had stocked up right before the ban, there's a chance that homes built after 1978 could have it.

Breathing or ingesting lead-based paint can cause serious health problems. Even if a home did have lead-based paint in 1978, there are likely to be at least a few layers of new paint over it, which largely addresses the issue. If you're planning on remodeling an older home, you'll want to take precautions when doing so. If you have small children, and they are prone to chewing on windowsills, you'll also want to be aware of lead-based paint under the surface. For most buyers, though, it's not an issue. If the cost of remediating it is high enough, it may not be worth it to do so. If you really want to know, an inexpensive test can be purchased at most hardware stores, and you'll have an immediate answer.

Asbestos—The sale of asbestos was also banned in 1978 (again, just the sale, so a home built after that may have asbestos from stock the builder had on hand). As with lead-based paint, it's not as big an issue as most people think. The most common uses of asbestos were in ceilings (popcorn, anyone?) and floor tiles. Just like lead-based paint, if you don't mess with it, it's not really an issue. If a home has it in the ceilings, leave them alone.

If you want to paint, strongly consider hiring a professional because too much paint may actually cause the asbestos material to break off. Alternatively, if you really believe popcorn should be limited to a movie snack, have a professional remove it for you. If the basement is tiled with asbestos, cover it with wall-to-wall carpet or flooring. There is also an easy test you can do to find out if that ceiling is really asbestos; not all popcorn ceilings are. Incidentally, asbestos was used prominently because of its fireproofing capabilities, so there is some benefit to having it in your home.

Radon—Radon is an odorless gas that is produced in the Earth's crust. It is a known carcinogen. It's very common in North Idaho and Eastern Washington. Levels are usually higher in basements so it's especially important to address it if you spend a lot of time in your basement. Radon can also be present in ground floors as well, so be sure to have your home tested by a professional. (There are home test kits, but they are not as precise as the equipment the pros use.)

Unlike lead-paint and asbestos, it can't just be fixed with a coat of paint or carpet. (Radon is a microscopic molecule that will seep through just about anything.) The good news is, not every home will have it

15

(in fact, one home may have high levels and the home next door may have almost none). It's fairly inexpensive to mitigate though, typically a few thousand dollars. Be sure to do your research on contractors and find one who comes back to test your home after the work is done and will fix it if the levels are still too high.

The EPA also recommends conducting a test on your home every year or so, even after you've mitigated the problem, to make sure levels haven't risen to an unacceptable level.

Oil Tanks—Most homes built in the past few decades are heated with electricity or natural gas (or even solar panels), but there are still several homes that use oil stored in tanks, and the installation of these is still legal in most places. They're nothing to be terribly concerned about, and some people even prefer them. The biggest issue with oil tanks is when they've been replaced by one of the newer forms of heating and are no longer used. They can potentially corrode and seep any remaining oil into the ground. You'll want to make sure they've been properly decommissioned.

If you have an active heating oil tank, you'll want to get it insured since many homeowners' policies don't cover them and the cost of cleaning up an oil spill can be as pricy as $100,000.00 (potentially even more, depending on what damage has been done to neighboring properties). In Idaho, you'll need to contact the Petroleum Storage Tank Fund (www.idahopstf.org). In Washington, contact the Washington Petroleum Liability Insurance Agency (plia.wa.gov). The cost for this insurance is minimal ($25 per year in Idaho; free in Washington), but it does not transfer to the new homeowners, so they will need to reapply.

One other thing buyers should know about oil tanks, just before closing, the oil company will measure how much oil is remaining in the tank so the seller can charge the buyer at the current price of oil. If you're the buyer, don't be alarmed when you see that cost on your closing statement. That's oil the seller didn't get to use and the buyer will so, naturally, the buyer should be paying for it.

Septic Tanks and Wells—Many homes built outside urban areas and even some older homes that may be surrounded by a sewer or water district, can have septic tanks and/or wells. Like everything above, properly maintained or addressed, they are nothing to fear and may even save you money over the long run. The key is to have them inspected before purchasing the home (in some jurisdictions, this is required of the sellers) and keeping them regularly maintained. A septic system properly maintained can last 50 years or more. (I've had septic inspectors tell me they've even found systems in good working order that were nearly a century old, although that's exceptional.) Septic and well inspections are conducted by inspectors specialized in those fields, so they will be done separately from your general home inspection.

OTHER ITEMS TO KEEP IN MIND BEFORE LISTING YOUR HOME

Home Warranties—Even if you're planning on getting your home pre-inspected and repairing every item on the list, you might consider getting a home warranty. These policies can cover the home for the time it's on the market until the transaction closes and will cover almost anything that might break (appliances, furnaces, plumbing, etc.) during that period.

Extended coverage can also be purchased for the new owners, so they'll have peace-of-mind in case any issues not discovered during the inspection come up, or their kid decides to flush his G.I. Joe down the toilet the day after they move in. There's typically a small service fee associated with each call and these policies typically cost a few hundred dollars per year but are well worth it.

Transferrable Warranties—If you replaced your roof, it probably came with a warranty. Your appliances, furnace, water heater, garage door, and many other items, including services you had done in your home, probably also have warranties. Find these warranties and receipts in that kitchen junk drawer and make a folder to give to the new owners. They will thank you for it if the water heater breaks.

Leased Equipment and Service Contracts—You may have items attached to your home which you don't actually own. Typically, this is your alarm monitoring system (although most alarm companies never want their panels back), but it may include your water heater, other appliances, or the pest control guy that comes out and sprays a few times a year and gave you a good deal because you signed up for a three-year service plan. Be sure to notify these companies that you're selling the home and arrange to pay off any early termination penalty and return any equipment if necessary.

Water and Power—This typically isn't something anyone thinks about, but if you've already moved out, and your home is going to be vacant, be sure you haven't cancelled water and electrical service. People viewing your home like to see it, quite literally, in its best light, and they'll sometimes turn on the water to check the water pressure. Of course, when an inspection is done, either by the home inspector or the appraiser, they'll also want to make sure water and power are working.

STAGING

Now that you know your home is in good working order, you should consider making it look as nice as possible.

This is what most people think of when they think of staging.

If your home is priced and marketed right and you don't have the money to pay for staging, it's not critical to the sale of the house. You'll probably still get a great offer and be pleased with the price you ultimately sell for, but it's still worth considering, especially in a slower market.

Most people want to sell for as much as they can and there are things owners and their agents can do to increase the chances of selling a home for a higher price even in a great market. Staging is one thing that consistently offers a great return on investment. In metropolitan markets like Seattle, it's almost a necessity and owners may spend thousands of dollars to do so.

Here in North Idaho, buyers aren't expecting that level of staging, so you're probably okay to do very minimal staging or even none at all. With more and more buyers coming from the larger metropolitan areas, though, many will be more likely to put an offer on a home that has been nicely staged. More people putting in more offers means your home will sell faster and for more money.

Furthermore, the overwhelming majority of buyers start their search for a home online, and if the home doesn't look good in photos, they may not look at in person it at all.

Before I go into what staging entails, here are a few facts about it:

- The return on investment for staging is, on average, more than 500%. (bankrate.com)
- Staged homes, on average, sell 88% faster and for 20% more. (realtor.com)
- 97% of buyers' agents said staging affects the buyers' view of the home. (NAR)
- Homes staged prior to going on the market sell on average, in 90% less time. (Real Estate Staging Assoc.)

- 58% of buyers' agents said staging increases the dollar value of the home. (NAR)
- Buyers view a home, on average, for six minutes and form an opinion in the first 15 seconds, but they'll linger in a furnished home an average of 40 minutes. (NAR)
- 27% of buyers are more willing to overlook property flaws in a staged home. (NAR)
- 81% of buyers find it easier to visualize a property as a future home when it's staged. (NAR)
- 78% of expired listings are vacant (of furniture). (NAR)

Now, some good news: staging may not be as expensive or complicated as you think. Staging actually entails much more (or less, depending on how you look at it) than bringing in a bunch of furniture. In fact, staging your home properly may not even require you to bring in any furniture at all, maybe just a few accessories.

It starts with decluttering and depersonalizing. When potential buyers walk into your home, they want to envision it as *their* home.

First, your home should be clean and organized. This goes beyond just vacuuming and picking up the papers on your desk. You'll likely need to remove some things, including, perhaps, some furniture. This is the time when you want your home to look as big as possible, so removing knickknacks, that wall of photos and other artwork, and the *extra* chair in the living room, will really open it up. Channel your inner Marie Kondo.

You should also do this in your closets. You may have your clothes packed in like sardines and the next owner may do the same, but fewer clothes, hanging neatly, will make the closet look bigger. Besides, anything you pack now, you won't have to pack later when it's time to move!

You'll also want to depersonalize the space. As much as you may love a particular sports team, and as silly as it may seem, that memorabilia you have hanging on the wall may be the thing that causes a buyer to walk away. Some people take their teams very seriously. (Can you imagine a Red Sox fan walking into a home decorated in a Yankees motif?) While there will likely be another buyer, the more buyers interested in the property, the higher the price you're likely to get.

If your furniture is dated, dirty, or worn, it should probably go into storage (or, at least, the garage, which buyers are more likely to disregard as cluttered even when stacked with a bunch of moving boxes). It may seem silly, but that old lounge chair that's been scratched up by the cat can bring down the whole mood of the room (as well as the home) and turn off potential buyers. You may like that your home looks lived in and homey, but most buyers want a clean slate on which to envision their plans.

Beyond all that, staging may mean painting or getting new carpet. I once saw a home that was owned by an eccentric artist and every surface of the kitchen was painted in wild colors and designs. The counters looked like a watermelon! I thought it was pretty cool, but even I wouldn't have wanted to live in a home like that every day, nor would the average buyers. They'd be thinking about the time and money they'd have to immediately spend to repaint it and reconsidering if this was the home for them.

While all rooms need to be clean and organized, not all rooms need to be staged. If you're moving out before you list your home, it's fine to leave most bedrooms vacant. Typically, you only need to stage the living room, family room, dining room, and master bedroom. You may be able to use a lot of your own furniture and just have the stager add some accents like pillows (stagers *love* pillows), neutral artwork (that stuff you see in an IKEA catalog), and hand towels in the kitchen and bathroom. These accents may only run you a few hundred dollars, but they can do wonders to brighten up a drab room with some color, or draw the buyers' eyes to a specific feature, which could end up netting you thousands of dollars more.

So, as with everything, you, the seller, are the boss. The choice is entirely yours. You don't need to stage a home, especially in a competitive market, and the extra effort and cost may not be worth it. But staging typically does net sellers much more than they spend, especially if staging consists mostly of taking out a lot of the clutter and extra furniture in your home and doing the small things like putting down fresh lining paper in the kitchen cabinets.

CURB APPEAL

Somewhat related to staging is curb appeal. This might be considered the staging of your yard, especially your front yard. They say you never have a second chance to make a first impression, so curb appeal is hugely important. I've had buyers turn around before they even get out of the car because the home didn't look appealing. This actually might have been their loss since the inside of the home might have been a real gem, and it wouldn't have taken much effort to clean up the yard.

What are some things to consider with curb appeal? Make sure everything is neat and tidy. Mow the lawn regularly and trim the hedges. If the season is right, plant some brightly colored flowers or hang some baskets of plants. Don't park your cars in the driveway, if possible. Get a new welcome mat. If you can't afford to paint the exterior of your home, at least paint the front door if it is scratched or chipped. (Even if the door is in good condition, you might want to paint it a brighter color to add more light to the entry.)

Pressure-wash your driveway and walkways. (Pressure washing is like a teeth cleaning for the home.) Even though the front yard is the most important part of curb appeal, you'll want to do some of these things in the backyard as well. Since most people spend more time in their backyards than their front yards, they will be critiquing it as another living space.

Lastly, if you're on good terms with your neighbors and they could use a little curb appeal themselves, you might want to delicately offer to pay for a little of their maintenance as well. A team I was part of once paid to have a neighbor's home painted because it was in rather poor shape. You might even frame the conversation around letting them know that the more your home sells for, the more their home will be worth. (This may or may not be a plus if they have no plans to sell, and they aren't wild about seeing their property tax go up.)

CLEANING

After you've taken care of all repairs and had your home staged, hire a professional cleaning service, including someone who will clean carpets, blow out your air ducts, and wash your windows inside and out. There's probably no better investment than this when preparing your home. Of course, you could do it yourself, but after everything else you've had to do, you'll probably be pretty exhausted. Let someone else make your home sparkle.

REMODELING

Taking on big projects before you list your home in order to make it shine is generally not advisable. In most cases, you won't get back what you invested into it. Furthermore, what a seller may consider an upgrade may not be what the eventual buyer likes.

One remodeling contractor told me that he once completed a $150,000 kitchen remodel. A couple years later, he was hired by the new owners to come in and completely remodel that same kitchen. It could be that the sellers didn't anticipate moving so quickly, and they did it for themselves, but it's worth noting.

In general, the only remodeling projects you should take on are really just more extensive repairs. These extensive repairs may end up turning into full remodels if you end up completely replacing and upgrading an old item. This would be wise if doing so doesn't cost much more than putting a few band-aids on the original problem. (As an example, would you spend $5000 to paint your whole house, extending the life of the siding by five years, or would it be smarter to spend $7000 on new siding that is going to last 30 years?

Before my family sold our last home, we decided to replace the entire deck. It was old and worn. While it wasn't a safety hazard by any means, the rest of our home really shined. We decided to spend the extra money to make the deck shine as well. Even with that project, though, we replaced it with a wood deck instead of a composite because there was significant cost savings in the short term. Had we planned on staying, we probably would have chosen composite.

If you are thinking of remodeling, kitchens and baths usually net the biggest return (although still far from 100%). Other things that actually do provide a decent return are replacing a roof (107%), new wood flooring (106%), new garage door (95%), and HVAC replacement (85%). (These statistics were taken from the National Association of Realtors 2019 Remodeling Impact Report and may have changed since then.) If these things are looking or working poorly, instead of just fixing them, you might want to consider replacing them all together. Most buyers want a turn-key home and will pay a little more knowing they won't have to replace the furnace a few months after they move in.

Lastly, remodeling might be as simple as installing all new handles and knobs on kitchen and bathroom cabinets or new faucets in all the sinks. This is relatively inexpensive and something even the least handy among us can generally do in a few hours.

As always, be sure to consult with a contractor and get a rock-solid bid on any project you're going to take on.

CHAPTER 3
GETTING YOUR HOME
READY TO SELL *ON PAPER*

TITLE - WHAT ARE YOU ACTUALLY SELLING?

Now your home is hopefully in tip-top shape. Everything has been repaired. You've slapped on a new coat of paint, and a stager has come in and made it look like something out of *Architectural Digest*. But you're not actually selling your home. At least not as far as the county government is concerned. You're actually selling your title to the home.

When your home finally closes, the title company will send a document called a deed over to the county recorder's office, informing them that you are no longer the owner of a particular parcel of land. Someone else is. That parcel of land isn't even your address. It's a legal description that will probably read something like "Lot 4, Block 2, according to the Plat of SUNSET MEADOWS, recorded in the office of the County Recorder in Book "C" of Plats at Page 89, records of Kootenai County, Idaho." (Imagine if you had to tell someone sending a postcard to write that on the back!)

Because you're selling that title, you'll need to make sure it's "clear and marketable". First, are you actually listed on it and allowed to sell it? Seems pretty basic, but sometimes mistakes are made, and if you've lived in that home for a long time, it might not be that simple. Maybe you inherited the home from someone, and that transfer was never recorded so that person, long since deceased, actually still owns it as far as the county is concerned. Or maybe you divorced several years ago, but never took your spouse off the title. (Let's hope you're still on fairly good terms since this happens more often than you might think.)

EASEMENTS & ENCROACHMENTS

Beyond that, does the title and plat map accurately indicate what you're selling?

The property I grew up on had an encroachment. The neighbors, way back in the 1930s, had built a boathouse near the property line and the chimney attached to it actually went over the property line a few inches. Our neighbors and we were friendly, so no one cared, but this sort of thing might be an issue to someone else.

In addition to encroachments, there might also be easements on your property that your neighbor benefits from or one on your neighbors' property that you benefit from. An easement is land that one person owns but allows someone else to use. The most common example of this is a utility easement, where the water or power company runs its pipes or power lines through your property. These you won't even notice. Another common one that may be a bit more of an issue is a driveway. If your property is surrounded by other properties and has no access to a public road, you'll need an easement to access it. These are usually recorded so everyone knows and adheres to the agreement. Sometimes, though, just as was the case with our neighbor and his chimney, it's not recorded and it's just a friendly agreement. That's fine until new owners come in and decide they don't want to allow you to use part of their property.

Another example of an encroachment might be a fence that was built six inches on your neighbors' side of the property line. If you get new neighbors who don't like that, they may force you to move the fence if it was never recorded on the title. If an encroachment or easement isn't recorded, it's best to do so. That way, any new owners going forward will know what the deal is.

One final example that's a bit obscure is air rights. (I could give others, but this will give you an idea of how obscure and overlooked some property rights can be.) When you buy a parcel, unless recorded otherwise, you own the land plus everything below it, going down to the center of the earth (which might be important if you're buying a mining or oil claim), and everything above it going into the stratosphere.

The home behind the one you're buying might have a really nice view, and the owners may love it so much that they want it protected. They may have made an agreement with the owners of the home you're buying to purchase the air rights so no one can add a second level and block the view. If you sell a home where this isn't disclosed, and the new owners bought it thinking they'd add a second level, someone is going be upset.

The above scenarios aren't very common, but they occur enough that you want to make sure, as the buyers or the sellers, you're aware that they might exist. They should all be recorded on the title if they do. A good real estate agent will make you are aware of these potential issues and then refer you to the title company or an attorney if you have questions, since they're the experts. As I mentioned above, some things may not be recorded on the title (like the fence built on the wrong side of the property line), so you'll want to make sure those have been addressed as well. If you think there may be some complicated issues related to your property's boundaries, you may even consider paying for a survey. These can be quite pricey though, even for a smaller lot, so you only want to have one done if absolutely necessary.

ZONING

The title and associated county records will also let you know about the zoning. Maybe your neighbors can't prevent you from adding a second level, but the city or county may have it zoned so that buildings can only be a certain height. Zoning may also address things like the size of your home or what percentage of the land it can cover.

I once represented a buyer who was in a backup position (meaning someone else had their offer accepted and my client was first in line if that deal fell through). The first buyers walked away because they wanted to build another set of stairs to a balcony. The home was already at its maximum lot coverage (of impermeable surfaces), so they walked away and my client was able to buy his dream home.

One more thing that zoning often addresses and might be of particular concern to buyers in North Idaho is how many and what kind of animals may be permitted. A couple of dogs or cats is almost always okay, but many areas won't allow things like chickens or other farm animals, even if it seems like the property could accommodate them.

LIENS

Title will also address any liens you might have against your property. The most common lien is your mortgage. The bank probably owns a significant portion of your property if you haven't lived there long or have recently refinanced. They're going to want to be paid back when you sell.

There might be other liens you haven't thought about. Someone may have done work on your home and didn't get paid. Thankfully, a "mechanic's lien" typically only remains on title for a relatively short time, and hopefully you do know about it since you probably received some kind of nastygram in the mail. But sometimes mistakes happen.

I once read a news story about a bank that foreclosed on a property. It reached the point that they'd sent the sheriff out to kick the owners off the land. The problem? The bank—and apparently everyone else involved—had mixed up a number on the address and were foreclosing on the wrong property. I'm not sure how this even happened, since addresses mean nothing, it's the legal description of the lot that matters. But there you go. The owners ended up suing the recalcitrant bank, and even sent a sheriff to its headquarters to enforce a lien against their property when they refused to adhere to the court order! Ah, sweet justice…

HOAs and CC&Rs

Homeowner's Associations (HOAs) and their CC&Rs (Covenants, Conditions, and Restrictions) are also a common item that will be recorded. These are very important to pay attention to, and unfortunately, they can sometimes rival *War & Peace* in their length. They may address things like what color you can paint your home, whether you can store your boat or RV in the driveway, the length of your grass, and whether you can rent out your home, either short-term or long-term. These may be of utmost importance to you.

One thing to keep in mind; you may read that RVs are not allowed to be stored in your driveway, yet you see several RVs parked in driveways. Don't think that they don't enforce their CC&Rs. When you buy your home, they might not, but a new president may be elected to the HOA board and might start cracking down and issuing fines.

CONDOMINUMS

HOAs and CC&Rs are especially critical when buying a condominium, so pay extra attention to all the documentation you're given to read when you enter into a contract to buy a condo. The CC&Rs, will probably include things like quiet hours, pets, what you can store on your balcony, and other things that contribute to a harmonious community when people are literally living on top of each other.

You'll also want to look at the Resale Certificate, budget, reserve study, and recent meeting minutes. These documents will tell you what's going on with the condo complex, how much money it has in reserve (in case something big happens, like the roof needing to be replaced), and what issues might be coming up. Condominium associations seem to be involved in lawsuits more often than might seem reasonable. You'll want to review meeting minutes to see if a lawsuit is being discussed so you can decide whether or not you want to be a part of the impending circus.

PROPERTY TAXES & CHARGES

Other things that will be public record, and you'll want to be aware of, are taxes and other charges. There are property taxes, of course, but there also might be a sewer capacity charge (something that's levied when a home hooks up to a municipal sewer but is paid off over the course of several years, usually 15, and then goes away) or

Local Improvement District levies or LIDs, which might be levied for road resurfacing or a traffic island or streetlights. These are levied once and then paid off. When buying or selling a home, you'll want to agree on whether the seller will pay these off before closing or if the new owner will assume them.

SCHOOL DISTRICTS & NEIGHBORHOOD AMENITIES

You'll also want to know what school district you're in and what other neighborhood amenities there are, so you can highlight them in your marketing (assuming it's a sought-after school district). Related to that, sellers might also want to highlight crime statistics if they're low. Buyers will probably want to know about them, especially if they're high. On that last point, you may also want to check the local sex-offender database (typically located on the local sheriff's website), if that's of concern to you as a buyer.

TENANT RIGHTS

If you're selling a rental property, you need to be aware that your tenants have rights. The lease you have with them supersedes any real estate contract, meaning, whomever purchases the property will have to honor that contract. This may be a plus if the person buying your home is also an investor and plans on renting it out. If the buyer wants it as their own home, however, consider asking your renters if they'd be willing to move out early and perhaps compensating them in some way to do so.

SHORT SALES & FORECLOSURES

Short sales and foreclosures have been a relative rarity since the market crash of 2008 and in a typical market, they don't make up a significant percentage of home sales. If you are in a position where you owe more on your mortgage than your home is worth, or worse, you can't keep up with the payment, my sincerest sympathies. That is a difficult place to be in. There are options, though.

You probably don't need to declare bankruptcy. If you haven't fallen too far behind on your payments, the bank will likely work with you to "short sale" your property. This means you can sell your property for what the market dictates, and the bank will accept that as the loan payoff amount. It's a bit of a complicated process, since the bank will have to approve any sale. It can be done though, and an experienced real estate agent will be able to assist you. You definitely want to explore the option of a short sale as early as possible to prevent your home from being foreclosed on, a process that means the bank has essentially repossessed your home.

For buyers, finding a home that is subject to a short sale or a foreclosure can be a great way of getting a deal. (And don't feel like you're a shark circling blood in the water by buying a short sale home. You're typically helping the owner out of a tight spot.) There are additional things to know, though. The bank will have to approve a short sale, and with a short sale or a foreclosure, the home is probably being sold "as-is." You likely won't be able to ask for any repairs.

"I found happiness in my own back yard, but my neighbor claims it's on his side of the property line."

CHAPTER 4
MORE PAPERWORK!

When you sell your home, invest in one of those little squeeze balls. You're going to be filling out a lot of paperwork, so your hands will thank you! (Well, hopefully, your agent will fill out most of the paperwork and you'll just have to sign it. But still, there's a great deal of paperwork!)

THE AGENCY DISCLOSURE BROCHURE

The first thing you'll sign, provided you're hiring an agent, is the Agency Disclosure Brochure. This details your rights (and a few responsibilities) as a customer or client (there's a difference) of the real estate brokerage. It discusses different forms of representation (Exclusive Right to Sell, Dual Agency, etc.).

It also covers some things to look for when hiring an agent and some things your agent must do and cannot do. It is fairly self-explanatory, but you'll want to review it with your agent and ask any questions you might have. Your agent should give this to you at your first meeting. Signing it just means you acknowledge receipt. It doesn't mean you've hired the agent.

SELLER REPRESENTATION AGREEMENT

If you decide to *hire* an agent to help sell your home, you'll sign a Seller Representation or Listing Agreement. I italicized *hire* because you typically won't pay an agent anything until your home actually closes. This might sound like a pretty sweet deal to you, and honestly, it is. That's part of the reason you need sign an agreement. While the agreement is mostly for your benefit, if you're selling a home, you don't have a choice as to whether you sign it or not. An agent can't legally sell your home without an agreement.

The key parts of this contract are the price you're going to list your home for, the term (days) of the contract, and your agent's compensation. Typically, this compensation is based on a percentage of the final sales price and is entirely negotiable. The agreement may also include a pre-determined amount you're willing to pay the buyers' agent who brings the buyer although this can also be discussed later as part of the eventual purchase and sales agreement. Finally, it may include things of note regarding showings, like what hours you don't want it shown or whether you want your agent to be there for all showings.

BUYER REPRESENTATION AGREEMENT

When you hire an agent to help you find a home, they will ask you to sign a buyer representation agreement. Like the seller representation agreement, this will outline their compensation. Oftentimes, your buyers' agent will negotiate their final compensation as part of the final purchase and sales agreement, but you and your agent may also agree that you'll compensate them separately, either at closing or in some other way like an hourly amount or a set retainer for their services. Whatever method you choose, it is completely negotiable between you and your agent.

As part of both the buyer and seller representation agreements, your agent, as well as you, are expected to act in good faith. If you feel your agent is not doing a good job, you are free to cancel that representation agreement on the spot. You are generally not locked in. The only time you might be locked in is if you've already gone under contract on a home purchase or sale. Even then, if your agent is not providing you the service you expect, there are things that can be done.

Typically, if there is a problem that can't be resolved between you and your agent, your agent's broker (who you technically have the agreement with), will reassign you to a new agent in the same brokerage. If your problem is with the whole brokerage, getting out of your listing contract may be more difficult, but still doable, if you can show that the brokerage is not performing adequately.

TRANSACTION FORMS

These next forms won't come into play until the offer process, but your agent should review them with you beforehand, so you know what to expect and won't have the added stress of figuring out what they all mean when you're under a deadline. The most common forms and items covered by these forms are as follows:

- **Purchase and Sales Agreement**—This is the most important form in the transaction. It will lay out:
- Parties to the Transaction (Agents, Sellers, and Buyers)
- Legal Description of the property
- Purchase Price
- Buyers' Financing

- Earnest Money (the amount and how it will be transmitted and handled)
- Closing Date
- Title and Escrow Company
- Title Insurance
- Inspection Contingency
- Closing Date
- Possession Date
- Walk-Throughs
- Other Terms of the Agreement
- Definitions

(In Washington, some of these items are covered by separate addenda)

- **Property Condition Disclosure**—Sellers have an obligation to disclose to buyers certain items about their property that buyers will likely want to know. These could be things like a leaky roof, past pest invasion, flooding, issues with any appliances that will be included with the sale, issues with plumbing or electrical, and zoning issues. These are not things the sellers are required to research, but if they do know about them, they are required to disclose them. Buyers beware, though. Unfortunately, whether because sellers simply aren't aware of an issue or they are being dishonest, not all issues covered by the Property Condition Disclosure may be disclosed. It is up to buyers to hire an inspector to uncover potential issues with the home they are purchasing. (Note that it only applies to properties with homes on them. Vacant land sales do not need to include one. Estate sales, where the property was not occupied by the sellers' representative also do not require a filled-out disclosure, the idea being that someone who didn't live there probably doesn't know much about the property.)

- **Escalation Notice**—In a strong sellers' market, buyers may end up paying more for a home than the list price. They certainly don't want to pay more than they must though, so they can include an Escalation Notice (referred to as an Escalation Addendum in Washington), which will tell the sellers that they are willing to beat the next highest offer by a specific amount of money up to a certain price.
- There are several other forms that cover uncommon transactions, like 1031 Exchanges, Sight Unseen Waiver, Assignment of Buyers' Interest, Delayed Possession, and Rental Agreements. If there's a situation that might come up, there's likely a form for it. If there's not a specific form, there's a blank addendum that can be filled out with particulars of a transaction.

  Buyers and sellers should be aware, though, that filling out blank addenda could be treading into slightly dangerous territory. Real estate agents are not lawyers and are not supposed to practice law. The definition of practicing law can vary, though. Some agreed upon issues may be easily covered in a sentence or two, but if any disagreement arises over what something written on a form means, a costly legal battle may ensue. At the very least, one party will probably be upset. Therefore, if there's any doubt over how an agreement should be worded, it is best to contact a real estate attorney.

41

CHAPTER 5
PRICING YOUR HOME

PRICE VS. COST VS. VALUE

Before I go into how to price a home, I want to cover the difference between price, cost, and value. Many people use these words interchangeably, and in most cases, we know what they are referring to. But these three words have distinct meanings that are worth (no pun intended) knowing.

The *price* of something is the actual dollar figure (or other item of value, like sheep or chickens in days of yore). It could be ridiculously high or low in relation to the cost and/or value, i.e. an art piece consisting of a banana duct-taped to a wall selling for $120,000, or a winning lottery ticket.

The *cost* of something is how much raw material, both physical, like bricks and windows, and manpower, went into it. With a home, unless the seller is a non-profit (by choice or just because they're not very good with money), the cost will be less than the price.

The *value* of something is the least definable. It's what someone *feels* the home is worth. In a really strong sellers' market, buyers may value a home far beyond its cost or price. I once spoke to an agent who ended up selling a home for more than 50% above asking price (and it was a very expensive home to begin with, so 50% above asking was *real* money!) It was a unique home and two different buyers wanted it a lot! They *valued* it far beyond its price or cost. Value often comes down to something subjective, but it can also be figured more objectively. If someone is buying a vacant lot with the aim of subdividing it and building ten homes, they probably have a good idea of how much those homes are going to cost to build and how much they will sell for. Taking the final sales price and subtracting the cost of development and the desired profit will tell the buyer what the objective value of the property is. Of course, the desired profit in this instance is a bit subjective since everyone values their time and expertise differently.

Knowing these three terms can help in pricing a home.

SUPPLY & DEMAND

Like everything else, the housing market follows the Law of Supply and Demand. If you're considering selling your home, and even if you aren't, you probably have some idea of what the housing market is doing since everyone seems to love to talk about real estate (or maybe it's just because I'm a real estate agent that people love talking about real estate to me).

It's all fine and good to have a general idea of what the market is doing, but if you're going to put your home on the market, you want to know within a few thousand dollars or so what your home is worth. There are many tools employed to come up with an answer, but the first thing you probably want to know is just how strong, either for buyers or sellers, the real estate market is specifically. That's determined by the absorption rate, which puts a number on that supply and demand. It's the amount of time it would take for all the homes on the market to sell if no new ones were listed. If your home is priced and marketed correctly, this is about how long it should take for your home to sell. Here's how you calculate it:

Total # of Sales/12 Months = Avg Sales/Month

Current # of Homes for Sale/Avg # of Sales/Month = Absorption Rate (Given in months)

It should be noted that, to get the best idea of the absorption rate for your home, you should use the current number of homes like yours. Clearly, a $12 million lakefront mansion is going to take longer to sell than a $450,000 house, so the more similar the homes are to yours, the better.

If you're selling a house, don't look at condos or manufactured homes. Look in a comparable price range (say, 10-25% above and below what you think your home is worth). Look in the same neighborhood as much as possible. There is a trade-off, of course. The more homes you input into the equation, the better idea you'll have of the market overall, but the less relevant to your specific situation it will be. Using that $12 million home as an example, if only two other homes have sold for more than $10 million in the past year and one was sitting on the market for two months, and the other took two years, it's really anyone's guess how long it will take for the $12 million home to sell or even if it's really worth $12 million.

The above process is what is known in the industry as a Comparative Market Analysis (CMA). In Idaho, where the final sales price isn't public record as it is in Washington, the final price can only be found by someone who has access to the Multiple Listing Service (MLS), so unless you're working with an agent who has this access, your CMA won't be as accurate. This is especially true in a market where homes may be selling for considerably more or less than the asking price.

Even when your agent has done a CMA, it can still be somewhat of a challenge to arrive at a good listing price. It's just as much an art as it is a science. For one, the housing market is constantly moving due to a myriad of factors, many of them somewhat unpredictable, so the price your home was last month is not the price it will be next month. And it may be no small change.

In January of 2020, eight months before we listed our own home in the Seattle area and COVID-19 wasn't a concern outside of China, I remember looking at a market report that showed our neighborhood had increased a scant 3% year over year, (3% in a typical market is about average), whereas other neighborhoods and cities in the greater Seattle area had increased as much as 20%. It's a good thing we didn't decide to move that spring because, by the time I pulled another market report for my neighborhood in July, it had jumped to 14% year over year—11% in just a few months!

Knowing this helps correctly price your home, because when you do a CMA, you may have to research comparable sales (called "comps" in the industry) from a few months back, maybe even a year back, if there aren't many homes to compare yours to. But knowing the general trend of the market means that you can take that month's-old sales price and increase it by the average market increase to arrive at a better price.

You'll also need to adjust the number based on differences in your comps since few homes are exactly the same. (If you live in a planned community where all the homes are pretty much the same, the job of pricing becomes much easier, of course.) If you find a home that has sold that's very similar to yours but has an extra garage or has its original kitchen, but you updated yours, that's something you'll need to adjust for.

It might be something even less noticeable. Your home might be exactly the same as the one you're comparing it to, but there may be a tree nearby that perfectly shades your back yard during the hottest part of the day. Something like that might not add much, if anything, to the price of your home, but if you and your neighbor decided to list at the same time, and there was only one buyer, it might be the deciding factor, so it's worth keeping in mind (and maybe even pointing out in the marketing).

BEING OBJECTIVE

Uniqueness can be a good thing. It makes every home more desirable to some extent because it's the only one there is. If two people really love it, they may even get into a bidding war, because unlike the buyer of a three-year-old Honda Civic, the loser can't just go to another dealership.

A potential downside to uniqueness, though, is that homeowners can become overly attached to their homes. A home can be like a member of the family. You've made it yours, and even if you're looking forward to moving to a new home, you're going to miss things about your old one. This probably makes you value it more than it's objectively worth, which is a big reason to hire a real estate agent. They don't have an emotional attachment to your home. They will be able to determine an accurate price much better than you will.

PRICE HIGH OR LOW?

That does bring up another point about pricing. In a strong sellers' market, it's always best to err on the side of pricing it a bit on the low side. Buyers will likely end up competing for your home and driving the price up, perhaps even higher than what you may have originally wanted to price it at. If you price it too high, though, you'll automatically eliminate some buyers, since people search in price ranges, and your home might be just above that range. If you price it too high, your home may also end up sitting on the market for too long, leading to a price reduction, and you'll end up getting even less than you would have had you priced it correctly the first time.

In a buyers' market, it's probably advisable to price it a bit on the high side, anticipating that you may only get one offer, it will probably be lower, and the buyers may try to negotiate the price down further after an inspection.

In a balanced market, you will have to analyze things a bit further. The fact is, there isn't really such a thing as a perfectly balanced market. If you read all the tea leaves correctly—the absorption rate, average days on market, the price of comparable properties—you'll have a pretty good idea of whether your individual neighborhood and price point will fall slightly in your favor or the buyers'.

When pricing a home, you're probably going to come up with a range of around 5%, meaning that a home that's worth $400,000 could reasonably be listed for anywhere between $390,000 and $410,000. In a sellers' market, you'll probably want to list it for $390,000. In a buyers' market, $410,000. It will also depend on how aggressive or cautious you want to be. If you need to sell your home fast and an extra $10,000 isn't that important, list low. If you don't mind waiting around a bit longer, list high. Keep in mind though, if you do list too high, the home may sit too long, and you'll end up getting even less than the low-end price.

PRICE ADJUSTMENTS AND
RE-MARKETING

"I think we need to drop the price." These are words no seller ever wants to hear, and no agent ever wants to utter. Both want to sell the home quickly and for the originally decided upon price. A price adjustment is even worse than it sounds in most cases because it means anyone who's been looking at it and not making an offer will smell blood in the water and descend like a shark, probably offering even less than the new price because they sense the seller is desperate. (Of course, sometimes there are enough sharks out there that they end up getting into a bidding war and driving the price back up, but that's more often the exception than the rule.)

So, when should you reduce your price? It depends on the overall market activity and the absorption rate I covered earlier. If the average home is going under contract with a buyer in three days and your home has been sitting for two weeks, there's probably something wrong; either the price or the way the home has been marketed. You can change up your marketing including, perhaps, staging the home differently or retaking photos.

If it's been sitting there for a while, you may have to change the price or do both things. Part of the reason is that most buyers cross a home off their list once they've seen it. Agents probably won't give it a second thought. Reducing the price will send out an MLS alert though, and it might raise their interest again. A good listing agent will also contact everyone who has previously looked at the home and let them know about the new price or new staging.

You'll also want to gauge showing activity. This might not make a difference on whether you reduce the price in the end, but it's useful to know. If your home has been sitting on the market for a long time, and you've had very few people viewing it, the price might be too high. But it also might mean the photos you've uploaded to the MLS are not showing your home in the best light (literally and figuratively).

You might also need to do more direct marketing, i.e. holding an open house if you haven't already, sending out postcards, doorbelling your neighborhood to ask if your neighbors know anyone who wants to move there, taking out an ad in the paper, etc., instead of just relying on the MLS.

If, on the other hand, your home hasn't received any offers but lots of people have been through it, you may want to look at the home again. Is it clean and organized? Is it staged nicely? Does it have a funny smell to it?! Before reducing the price, you'll want to make sure your home shows well in person.

If you do want to list your home on the high side and "test the market", it's probably a good idea to discuss a price reduction strategy in advance. Perhaps you will agree to drop the price $5000 after two weeks on the market and another $5000 every week after that.

REVERSE OFFERS

Maybe you think you've done everything reasonably possible to get your home ready to sell and you feel the price is right. Maybe you've even had a few potential buyers through but no offers. Buyers aren't the only ones who can make an offer. Sellers can make a "reverse offer". Someone might be wavering on making an offer and might just need the extra little push that comes from a seller picking up the phone and asking what it will take to make the buyer comfortable with the home. It might be the price, but it might be something else that the seller hasn't even thought of. They say half of success in life is just showing up. In this case, *showing up* can just be reaching out.

ONLINE PRICING

There are several websites that will tell you how much your home is worth. Your county assessor's site is one of them. There are also some private sector companies that do price valuations. They're all almost always wrong. With the assessor, this is a good thing, since they only make it around to your home every two years or so and housing prices typically go up. That means you're paying less in taxes than you would be if the assessor was constantly valuing your home.

Private companies that do this are also usually wrong, sometimes even more so than the assessor. Computers are great. They crunch big data much faster than a human ever could. The thing about computers though, they can't walk inside your home and look around (other than the ones in the dystopian movies that we won't talk about). They also all run the GIGO program—garbage in, garbage out. That means, if the county assessor's site that they're pulling information from says your home is 2000 SF, but it's actually 2500 because you finished an unfinished basement, the computer won't know. The computer also can't always differentiate between a home that's been remodeled and one in its original condition.

True story: one of those online sites once valued a listing of mine 200% over what it sold for. The crazy thing was, it was still valuing it at that astronomical figure a few weeks after the sale closed, which just goes to show you how often some of these sites update their price estimates. As much as I would have liked to sell that home for 200% more, I have a good suspicion as to why it was off. The home I sold was a hundred years old and hadn't been updated. Most of the homes in the neighborhood were of the same age and size, but had gone through full remodels so they were, essentially, brand new homes.

In short, don't pay any attention to what those online sites tell you.

NET PROCEEDS

It would be nice if the price your home sold for was the same as the dollar amount you found in your bank account the day after your sale closed. For those who don't have a mortgage, those numbers may be close, but there are still additional costs associated with selling a home beyond paying off your mortgage. So, your agent will prepare a "Seller Net Sheet" for you. This is still a bit of an estimate, but it should be within a hundred dollars of the final number. A few days before closing, the escrow company will give you what's called a HUD-1 Settlement Statement that should be exact so you can check it for any errors. Items included in this net sheet are:

- Mortgage Payoff
- Agents' Commission
- Excise Tax (this applies only in Washington, where it is currently levied at 1.78% of the sales price on most homes, although it can vary from 1.1% to 5% depending on the price of the home and the city where it is located.)
- Title Insurance Premium (the seller typically pays the larger portion of this; although who pays it is negotiable). If the buyer has a mortgage, a separate title insurance premium will be paid (typically by the buyer) covering the bank's interest in the property.
- Pro-rated property taxes
- Pro-rated homeowner association dues, if applicable
- Pro-rated utilities. Your water, sewer, and garbage service are typically tied to the property as well as the owner, meaning, if you skipped out on paying those bills, the new owner could be stuck with them. Your

final electricity and gas bill may also be paid out of escrow. Since these can vary, escrow will typically hold back more than what the bill will actually be and send you a refund for the difference after closing.

- Any other liens you may have on your property. This might be a bill for final repairs made during the closing period.
- Notary fee
- FIRPTA. What is FIRPTA, you ask? It may sound like the latest plush toy with big, cute eyes, but it's actually not cute at all. FIRPTA stands for the Foreign Investment in Real Property Tax Act. It's a federal law passed to tax realized gains by foreign investors in U.S. real estate. The tax rate is typically 10% of gains, but since the government doesn't know how much you bought the home for, how much you've invested in any remodels, etc., and how much you paid to sell it, the escrow company will typically hold back 15% of the sale price unless a withholding certificate is obtained from the IRS. (Of course, once the foreign seller completes their U.S. taxes at the end of the year, they'll get a portion of this back, but why wait?)

For buyers, FIRPTA is actually hugely important. Make sure, when you're purchasing a home, you have a FIRPTA addendum or some other language in your contract that absolves you of responsibility for paying the tax. Buyer paying the sellers tax, you say, shocked? No doubt! It seems horribly unfair, and it is, but if a foreign seller doesn't disclose their status and skips the country without paying FIRPTA taxes owed, the IRS is going to come after the low hanging fruit, and it's a lot easier to get money out of someone who currently owns a home in the U.S. than it is someone who is a foreign citizen residing in a foreign country.

"Our asking price is $699,000.
Our begging price is $58,000."

CHAPTER 6
FINANCING

If you're buying your next home with all cash, congratulations! Provided your offer is high enough to be accepted, the transaction process will be a breeze with a closing likely happening in less than a week. For the rest of you, you'll be securing a loan. Even if you have enough moncy to pay all cash, you may still want to get a loan, especially if the interest rate is low. When you get a loan, you're earning investment income in one form or another, not only on your own money, but on other people's money, as well.

Before we go into loan types, know that you'll need to get "pre-approved" for a loan. Pre-approved is different than pre-qualified. It means that you've submitted all your financial paperwork like pay, bank, and credit card statements to a loan officer and they've reviewed and verified them and obtained your credit score. Pre-qualified only means that you may have gone on a website, entered how much money you make and what your current monthly debt payments are, then received an amount you're "qualified" for. It essentially means nothing if the bank doesn't verify all this information.

When you are pre-approved, be sure to get a letter from your loan officer. When making an offer, they should send you one specifically tailored to the property with its address and the offer price as the limit. This will show the sellers you are professional. By only putting your offer price on it, it also won't tip your hand, letting the sellers know you could actually pay more.

When you go through the pre-approval process, your mortgage loan officer will tell you how much you qualify for, at what rate, and what type of loan is the best option for you. There are several kinds.

- **Conventional**—this is the most common and the one with the fewest hoops to jump through. Typically, a buyer will put down 20% (some conventional loans accept lower down payments, but Private Mortgage Insurance (PMI) will need to be paid). There aren't too many things to look out for with the bank appraisal for this loan. If the buyer is putting a considerable amount down, the bank may even conduct a "drive by" appraisal or waive it altogether.

- **FHA**—this is a loan underwritten by the Federal Housing Administration. This loan is for homes below a certain value (which changes depending on the year and the area of the country but is tied to the median value). An FHA loan allows the buyer to put a smaller percentage down, typically between 3.5% and 10%, depending on credit score. (PMI will still be required.) The appraisal and inspection are more stringent for someone with an FHA loan. For sellers, there typically isn't a huge risk involved in accepting an offer with an FHA loan, but if all else is equal, the conventional loan is the safer option, being more likely to close. FHA loans are also only available for owner occupied properties.

- **VA**—As a thank you to those who serve or have served in the military, the federal government offers loans underwritten by the Veterans Administration. These loans allow the buyer to put nothing down. Like FHA loans though, the appraisal and inspection are more stringent. A VA loan can be for an investment property or second home, but a borrower is only allowed to have one active VA loan at a time.
- **USDA**—the U.S. Department of Agriculture offers loans on properties that are in certain areas. These are often rural or farm properties, but some smaller towns in rural areas may also qualify, so a single-family home on a small plot of land may also qualify for a USDA loan. This allows for a smaller down payment.
- **Seller Financing**—If you can't get a loan from a bank, you might be able to get the seller to finance the purchase. Basically, the seller would be the bank. You may or may not put a certain percentage down, then you'd make monthly payments at an agreed upon interest rate to the seller. Unlike a more traditional loan, this will likely be a shortened time period, maybe five years or less, instead of thirty. This time will give the buyers a chance to build up equity in the property so that they can get a traditional loan and pay off the remaining balance. Seller financed mortgages are complicated contracts, so be sure to have an experienced professional review all paperwork.
- **Idaho Housing Authority**—this isn't a type of loan so much as it is a program for Idaho residents making under a certain amount of money to qualify for lower interest rates than they may be able to get elsewhere, as well as down payment and closing cost assistance and homebuyer tax credits. Check with your lender to see if you may qualify for this program. Washington and most other states have a similar program as well.

- **Closing Costs**—this isn't part of the loan, but it is
something buyers will have to pay before or at closing.
These may include, but is not limited to, appraisal fee,
mortgage lender's title insurance policy, escrow fee,
notary fee, and loan origination fee. Most of these fees
must be paid up front and can't be rolled into the
mortgage. If you are tight on money though, you can
ask the sellers to pay all or part of your closing costs.

WIRE FRAUD

If you remember nothing else from this book, remember
this: wire fraud is way more prevalent than it should be and
can be difficult to detect, even by people who clearly know
they haven't just inherited a million dollars from the
Crown Prince of Nigeria.

What makes wire fraud scams in real estate so
diabolical is that the scammers have so much specific
information and are pros at mimicking email addresses.
The way it typically works on their end is that they hack
into a real estate or title companies server and find out
when a deal is closing. They will have the names of the
parties, including the title officer and real estate agents.
They will have the amount being paid and pretty much
everything else related to the transaction. They will then
mimic an email from the title officer telling you that wiring
instructions have changed and to now send your down
payment to a new place. This new place might even be the
same bank, just a different account. (I still haven't found a
good answer as to why banks can't verify the account
name on the other end of the wire, but it is what it is.)

I've even heard that scammers have gone one step
further. Since they have your phone number, they'll call
you right after they send you an email and mask their
number, so it looks like it's coming from the title company.
Since you probably don't recognize the voice of your title

officer, you probably won't know it's not them. You're probably a bit stressed out and have been told to respond to all sorts of emails and phone calls from the title and mortgage companies promptly, so you do, and now you've wired the bulk of your life savings to Russia or wherever. Sometimes, if this is caught quickly enough (like, within minutes), the banks can reverse it. But usually, as soon as it hits one bank, it gets sent out to another and maybe another after that. Sadly, there usually isn't a way to get your money back.

So, now that I've thoroughly scared you, what can you do to not be a victim of wire fraud? If you get an email from your lender, real estate agent, or mortgage broker telling you to wire money to a different account, it's almost 100% likely that it's a scam. Call up whomever supposedly sent you the email to verify the information. Don't use the number in the email though. Use the number they gave you the first time you spoke or go to their website (again, type the URL in; don't click on any links in the email) and get their number from there.

The surest way to not fall victim to wire fraud, of course, is to just not wire money. This can be difficult if you're paying hundreds of thousands of dollars or time is tight, but you should be able to arrange to bring a cashier's check for your down payment to closing if you're more comfortable with that.

CREDIT SCORES

While we're on the subject of financing, here's a very brief run down on credit scores. Unsurprisingly, the better your score, the better interest rate you're likely to be offered. In general, to qualify for most loans, including the low-down payment FHA loan, you'll need at least a 580-credit score.

With a score below 620, you're considered "subprime" and a greater risk to lenders so you will likely have a much higher interest rate.

Above 670, you'll qualify for a good rate and should have no problem getting approved.

Above 750, you are considered to have excellent credit and will qualify for the best interest rates.

There are things you should keep in mind before applying for a loan and during the purchase process. If you're just starting out and haven't established much credit, you may want to consider getting a credit card with a low credit limit and using it regularly to establish some credit. An account like a cell phone can also help establish credit.

If you have established credit but it could be better, things you can do to improve it are paying off any late payments, paying down high balances, and paying off accounts. Improving your credit score can take time, but less time than you may think. Typically, if you pay off late payments and get your total credit balance down to a reasonable level, you can see significant change in as little as six months. Some lenders may even be able to do something called a "rapid rescore", where they rerun your credit after you've fixed some issues and get a more favorable picture of your financial situation.

One other thing you might do to improve your credit, which might seem counterintuitive is to ask for a credit limit increase on one of your accounts. By doing so, you will reduce the percentage of available credit being used and likely improve your score. Of course, people with "subprime" credit scores probably aren't going to get a loan limit increase, but if you're trying to go from just below 750 to just above 750, so you can qualify for a better rate, this might be a way to do it.

Before doing anything, you might think of to improve your credit, check with your mortgage loan officer or someone else who knows the mysteries of credit scoring. Something you might do that seems like it'd be a good idea, like closing an account, might actually lower your credit score, thereby raising the interest rate you're offered or denying you a mortgage altogether.

Of course, if you have something more drastic in your credit history, like a bankruptcy or foreclosure, that will take longer to fix, but know there is light at the end of the tunnel even with that.

Once you've applied for a loan, regardless of how good your credit is, don't make any changes to your financial profile. This means don't take on any new debts. Some people will be tempted, once they've entered into contract on a home, to go out and buy a bunch of furniture. Picking up an end table that costs $100 is probably fine, just don't go out and finance the entire living room set for $3000. Certainly, don't go out and buy a new car! Also, don't make any large cash withdrawals or deposits. The mortgage company is going to have to document all large transactions in your bank account. So, if your grandmother gives you a check for $5000, wait to deposit it. Don't do any of this until the process of buying your home is 100% complete. Banks are giving you a considerable amount of money and can change their minds at the last minute if they think you're going to be too big a risk.

When we bought our current home, we also bought two new cars better suited to our new climate. I did have to put a small deposit down to hold one of them, and I made sure that was okay with my mortgage loan officer. She was very clear, however, to not get the huge cashier's check we needed to buy the other car (even though we were paying cash), until after our home purchase had closed. We actually sat in our old car outside the bank waiting on a phone call from her to tell us we could go inside and get the cashier's check.

"The key to home buying is LOCATION. You'll need the money located in your savings account, you'll need the money located in your checking account, you'll need the money located under your sofa cushions..."

CHAPTER 7
MARKETING YOUR HOME

Your home looks better than it ever has before, so nice, in fact, you might be thinking you'd like to stay! You've reviewed all the legal paperwork and transaction forms. You're set! Now it's time to let the world know how amazing your home is. It's time to market!

THE MULTIPLE LISTING SERVICE

You'll most likely want your agent to upload your home to the Multiple Listing Service (MLS). This is a database of nearly all the homes for sale in your area. It is usually the way most homes end up selling. All homes in the MLS are also pushed out to a myriad of websites. Most brokerages have their own websites. You'll also find them on sites such as realtor.com and zillow.com.

A note about Realtor.com, Zillow.com, and probably a few other non-brokerage websites: they are powerhouses in the industry and have contributed positively to the industry in many ways. They are also generally accurate when it comes to active listings, but I have found that they can sometimes lag a day or two for some listings. So, if you see a home listed on Zillow or

Realtor.com, ask an agent with direct access to their local MLS to confirm that the home hasn't already gone under contract and that the price and features listed are also accurate.)

PHOTOS

Getting on the MLS is the most important thing you can do to market your home. After your home is on the MLS, the next most important thing is to provide good photos. If the words in a listing are the steak, the photos are the sizzle. This is not the time to go cheap and pull out the iPhone camera and DIY. Your home is now the *star* of this little production, and just like a Hollywood star, you want a great cameraman and great lighting.

I have a folder on my computer called "Bad Listing Photos". There are even websites out there that are devoted to such horrendous wonders. Sometimes photos make it into my folder or on to those websites because the subject of the photo just looks horrible. The owners didn't clean or stage their home, or they decided it wasn't worth it to replace the green shag carpet. I lost count of how many photos I've seen with laundry piled up on a bed! But often, there really isn't anything wrong with the home, which is tragic. Your home may shine in person, but if someone sees a poorly lit photo, they may pass on by and never go see it in person.

MLS LISTING DETAILS & DESCRIPTION

While photos are the first thing someone will likely look at on the MLS, make sure all the fields on the MLS are accurately filled out. These will help people narrow their search by certain criteria to find your home. If you have a view of the water, make sure your agent is checking the "water view" box, etc. Beyond that, take some time with the description. This is your chance to tell the story behind the story that the photos and check boxes don't show. Be creative! A well worded description might just catch the eye of someone flipping through listings and be the thing that sells your house.

SIGNAGE & KEYBOX

Beyond uploading your listing to the MLS, placing a For Sale sign in the yard is the bare minimum your agent should be doing. It can be effective in letting people who might be driving by know that the home is for sale. These drive-bys can actually be pretty effective in drawing traffic. Beyond that, they help people who already know about your home find it a bit more easily. If it's a difficult to locate property, like a vacant lot or piece of property located down a private road, you'll definitely want a sign, as well as some arrows, from the main road.

NEXT LEVEL MARKETING

While most homes are initially found by potential buyers through the MLS and the other websites that the MLS aggregates to, a good agent will go a little further and market your home in other ways.

- **Doorbelling**—neighbors can be a great resource. They may have friends or family looking to move to the area. By letting them know a nearby home is available, they can let those friends and family know. Your agent may even hold a special "neighbors only" preview open house.
- **Mailers**—Agents can send out "Just Listed" postcard to neighbors, other agents that work in the area, and lists of people who may be looking for a home like yours.

- **In-home marketing**—many buyers may be looking at several homes in a day and they can all start to blur together. To help point out key features, especially ones that may be overlooked like soft-close drawers in the kitchen or extra storage, agents should put up small signage around the home. They should also have a flyer that buyers can take with them that detail the particulars of the home and key features.

- **Open Houses**—some agents will say these are a waste of time, that no homes are really sold through an open house. I suppose a case could be made for this. After all, if someone sees your home online and really likes it, they'll probably make an appointment. But why not make things easier? They may be looking at several homes in a day and scheduling all these viewings can be difficult. If you have a time when they can drop by, it removes some of that hassle. I've sold homes to people who've come to an open house, so I know it works.

  A note to buyers: if your agent is busy and can't accompany you to an open house, that's okay. Just be sure to let the listing agent know you have your own representation. While most agents are honest and won't try to get you to use them to write up an offer, if you don't let them know you're working with someone, they might. This may not seem like a big deal, but remember, they are working for the seller and trying to get them the best deal possible. They contractually don't have *your* best interests in mind. Your agent will advocate for you.

- **Personalized websites, video, and virtual walk-throughs**—for nicer homes that have exceptional features (large lot size, or views), doing a video walk-through or drone photography/videography can really help sell your home, especially to those who may only be looking online because they live far away. The more you can show them online, the more likely they are to feel comfortable doing so. Having a personalized website for your home also helps publicize it to a larger market.

SHOWINGS

Your agent has marketed your home well and now people are wanting to come see it. As mentioned above, a great way to get them in is through an open house. Not everyone will want to or be able to come to an open house though, so they'll schedule a private showing.

These private showings are typically made through the listing agent and the buyers' agent. This helps the sellers from being bombarded with calls and lets the agent handle questions about the property. Sellers, you may want a call beforehand, but it's useful if you let your agent know when they don't have to contact you, like when you know you'll be at work or out of town.

For ease, a record of showings, and security, your home will probably be outfitted with an electronic key box. This is a nice little invention that makes it easier for people to show your home by allowing other agents with access to the system to retrieve a key. It also logs their entry so you know who's been in your home and for how long. (Agents are supposed to leave their cards behind and really should contact the listing agent after each showing, but sometimes fail to do so.)

Before you start accepting appointments for open houses or private showings, you need to prepare your home. Of course, you've already cleaned and staged your home, but if you're still living in it, make sure it is picked up, and any areas that have become dirty since the cleaning are cleaned again. Don't leave paperwork on your desk, run the vacuum over the carpet, and clean the kitchen counters one more time.

Secure any small and important belongings. Put jewelry in a safe and secure medications. Unfortunately, there are dishonest people out there and some of them will target homes for sale as a way to pocket small, but expensive items like prescription medication or jewelry when their agent isn't looking. If you're especially concerned about security, you may want to invest in a recording system. Just be sure to let people know they are being recorded. It's the right thing to do.

Lastly, in regard to preparing your home for a showing, some agents swear by baking cookies or bread right before an open house. At the very least, do make sure your home smells inviting but stay away from any strong-smelling scents that may actually irritate some people's noses.

In a strong sellers' market, most showings will occur the first few days your home is listed. It's worth considering taking a short vacation or staying in a hotel, so you won't have to constantly make sure your home is clean and picked up.

If you have tenants, in most jurisdictions, you're required to give them 24-hours' notice before a showing. (24-hours' notice is not always possible, so you should have a discussion with your tenants and ask them if they'd be willing to leave during showings on shorter notice.) Since they're the ones who will need to be keeping the home clean and vacating the property, you might want to incentivize their cooperation by offering them a discount on their rent during the time your home is on the market.

Once showings happen, the listing agent should be asking for feedback. A list of basic questions for viewers helps the agent determine the success of the showings.

- Is the price too high, too low, just right? Other agents see lots of homes and have their own opinions of what a home should be priced at. It's worth getting their and their clients' opinions. Your home may not work for a potential buyer, but they may still think it's fairly priced.

- What features did they especially like? If these haven't been included in the marketing, it may be worth adding them.
- What didn't work? Most of these things probably can't be fixed (small bedrooms, didn't have a view, etc.), but they're worth noting. There might be other things, though, that can be done to improve future showings.

If a bedroom does seem small, maybe some extra furniture just needs to be removed. Maybe you or your agent didn't spot something during the staging process, or you didn't think it would be a big deal. (I once showed a home that had an entire room wallpapered with movie posters. For a movie lover, that might have been fun, but it was too busy and distracted from the room. Some of the movie posters might have even been somewhat offensive to some people. The listing agent may have warned the seller about this, but sometimes a second opinion may help convince people of its validity.)

- What other homes are the buyers looking at? Sellers should definitely know their competition.
- Is the buyer willing to accept an offer from the seller? I mentioned the reasoning behind this above in the earlier section on reverse offers.
- At the very least, your agent should be keeping a record of all somewhat interested buyers. If you do end up dropping the price or doing something else to entice buyers, your agent will want to call that buyers' agent back to let them know to come back.

"You did a great job describing my house
in the Real Estate Ads. It sounds so appealing,
I've decided to keep it!"

CHAPTER 8
THE OFFER PROCESS

Before you start reviewing offers, you should prepare yourself mentally. In a strong sellers' market, that may mean multiple offers. This is usually a good problem to have, as it means your home will sell for more. But it can be a bit stressful when the key parts of an offer usually involve more than just price. Other parts of the offer you may have to consider could be financing options, down payments, inspections and other contingencies, closing periods, and even buyer positioning statements (sometimes called love letters), which I will cover shortly.

Know what you're looking for in an offer. It may be worth accepting a lower offer, pricewise, if the closing period is shorter or the buyers' financing is stronger (i.e., all cash vs. a conventional or FHA loan that could, potentially, fall through) or they've waived the inspection contingency. A bird in the hand is worth two in the bush, as they say.

In a buyers' market, you may need to wait awhile for an offer to come in. Discuss with your agent beforehand how long you're going to wait before you drop the price and how much you'll drop it by if that time comes. This way, you won't be making the decision under pressure.

OFFER GUIDELINES

In both types of markets, but especially in a sellers' market, you will want to write these offer guidelines down. Provide a gold standard for buyers to meet. They may be thinking you want to close quickly, since most people do, but you may be wanting to stay in your home if possible or rent the home back from the new owners after the sale. Unless you tell them, they won't know to offer this.

Perhaps you were burned on the last offer and the buyers' financing fell through, so you're very reticent about accepting anything other than conventional with 25% down. If you did a pre-inspection and didn't find any significant issues with the home, you'd probably want people to not include an inspection contingency in their offer. Or you could be feeling generous and are willing to pay a portion of the buyers' closing costs. On this last point, it could be that a buyer has great financing but is really scraping to come up with the down payment and the additional closing costs, which typically run about 2-3% of the purchase price.

So, what does a gold standard offer look like? Here's a good list to start with.

- **Price**—This most important thing for almost everyone. But it might not be the be-all and end-all. If you really just want to be over and done with the whole sales process, the sooner and easier it can close may make up for a considerable amount of money.
- **Inspection**—I advise all my sellers to get a pre-inspection, regardless of the type of market we're in. When offer time comes, this can alleviate a lot of concerns from potential buyers who may want to make

an offer, but not shell out another $500 for an inspection, especially if they've already done so a few times only to be beat by another offer or find something on inspection that causes them to walk away. If you include an inspection, buyers may still want to do their own, but this makes asking that they waive that contingency a lot easier.

Also, an inspection contingency is a "get-out-of-jail-free card". Buyers don't have to tell you that they're walking away because the hot water heater is 19 years old, or they found rats in the crawlspace. They can just tell you they're walking and there's nothing you can do about it.

- **Title and other contingencies**—buyers may have contingencies in place to review title and other paperwork. This might be fine and necessary, but how much better is an offer if they've already looked at all this paperwork, like title, and said they're good to go. Like inspection contingencies, some of these other contingencies don't necessarily require a reasonably defensible reason to back out.

- **Financing**—beyond inspections, this is the number one thing that will typically cause a transaction to fail before closing. First, every offer should include a pre-approval (remember, pre-*approved*, not pre-qualified) letter from a reputable mortgage broker (see below), or proof of funds if the buyers are paying all cash. If your home is especially nice, you may even want to weed out looky-loos by requiring their agents to provide a pre-approval letter before showing. You're selling your home, not participating in the Grand Tour of Houses.
  - **Type of financing**—not all financing is equal. Conventional is the best as it has the fewest hoops for the buyers to jump through.

- **Down Payment**—this might not seem like a big deal, but the more money buyers put down, the more likely things will go smoothly if issues come up. The most common time this comes into play is if the home doesn't appraise for value, meaning the bank's opinion of the home it is helping the buyer purchase is less than what the contract price is. If buyers were required to put 20% down to qualify for the loan but after the appraisal is done, it turns out the home isn't worth the purchase price and that 20% is now 18%, they can't buy the home unless the sellers come down in price.

  Other things could come up like buyers taking on additional debt during closing or interest rates rising. If they've said they're putting more money down in the beginning, these things might not cause a problem. If they're on the edge, they will. A larger down payment also shows they're financially stable. Someone who is stretching to afford a home may not really be able to afford it, and the loan officer is really just hoping things end up working out.

- **Loan Company/Loan Officer**—this isn't usually a big concern since loan companies are licensed and do a pretty decent job or they don't last long, but it is worth paying attention to. If you receive multiple offers, it might be the deciding factor. Things to look out for here are whether the loan company/loan officer is local. An out of state company (meaning all the loan officers work out of state, not necessarily that the company is just based out of state, but has local offices), may not know the local market and the local laws. An important zoning requirement or something like a septic inspection might get missed until the last minute and when it's noticed, the loan company may decide it doesn't want to fund the loan or things are going to be delayed until that paperwork is complete.

A lot of these out-of-state loan companies also often work banker's hours. If something comes up during the weekend or in the evening, you want to be dealing with a loan officer who will pick up the phone at 8:30 at night and do what they can to address the issue as soon as possible. To this end, make sure your agent is actually calling the loan officer personally and getting the story behind the story. The loan officers won't necessarily be able to disclose everything (although the buyers should have signed something stating they can), but they should be able to tell you and your agent a lot to help alleviate any concerns.

- **Earnest Money**—this is typically about 1% of the purchase price, but you may want to ask for more. Earnest money is insurance. If your buyers change their minds (maybe they get cold feet, maybe they find a home they like more), they may decide it's worth losing their earnest money to walk away. In Idaho, sellers can sue buyers for more than the earnest money if they can show that they've been harmed financially beyond that amount, but do you really want to go to court? Retaining existing earnest money is a lot easier than suing for extra. Earnest money is also a good indicator of financial stability.

You may even ask that some or all of that earnest money be converted to a non-refundable deposit, which means, if your buyers walk for any reason other than the sellers' failure to perform, the sellers get to keep the money. It's basically the same as having the buyer waive all remaining contingencies but has a bit more weight behind it. Earnest money is held by the escrow company.

- **Closing Costs**—The most solid offer should really have the buyer paying their own closing costs. (There are a few costs the sellers traditionally pay, like the sellers' portion of title insurance and the brokerage fee.) You may be feeling generous or want to entice buyers by offering to pay some or all of their costs. This can really help them out because these costs can't be rolled into their mortgage. They must be paid up front and can be thousands of dollars.

- **Closing period**—the sooner buyers can close, the sooner sellers will have the stress of selling their home behind them and have that big fat check in their bank account. It also means less can go wrong. (If someone loses their job the day after closing, that's their problem, as sad as it may be. If they lose their job the day before closing, it's both sellers' and buyers' problem.) A short closing period is also another indicator of financial stability and the fact that they were probably fully underwritten.

- **Rent-back**—in a strong sellers' market, while it can be easy for sellers to sell, it can be a challenge for them to find a new home so, as a seller, you may want to ask to rent your home back from the new owner for a short time. You may have found a new home but are waiting for it to close or you might be waiting for a new home to be built. Maybe you just want to spend one last holiday in your old home or wait until the end of the school year to move. All of these things can be accommodated by renting back.

In most cases, if the loan is financed as a primary residence, this time period is limited to 60-

days after closing. But if you need more time, buyers who really love your home may be able to obtain investment property financing for that period. That's a higher interest rate loan, but it might be worth it to them.

As a buyer, you should be somewhat cautious about entering into this situation. It'll probably be fine, but know that you're a landlord now, and it's your home. If the sellers, who are now your renters, decide to trash the home, you'll have to pay for it (whether through your own funds or a rental deposit you may have asked for). If your renters decide they don't want to move out, you must go through the eviction process, which is very difficult.

BUYER POSITIONING STATEMENTS

There's debate as to whether buyers should include positioning statements that give a narrative reason as to why their offer should be picked. The National Association of Realtors discourages it. Some agents warn sellers against reading them because they are afraid it might open the sellers up to a Fair Housing lawsuit, the thinking being that the letters may include information about the buyers that place them in a protected housing class (race, ethnicity, gender, age, family status, veteran status, sexual orientation, or sexual identity).

I disagree with this view. From my research, I've found many people warning against these letters for the above reason, but no record of any actual lawsuit. In this day and age of social media, if sellers really care about someone's protected status, they can find that information out pretty easily. I disagree partly for those reasons, but mostly because I don't believe most people are looking to discriminate, nor are most people looking for the next person to sue. Maybe it's a bit naive of me, but I choose to live life believing that most people are kind and generous unless they give me a reason to believe otherwise.

Furthermore, as a buyer, there's zero risk of being sued for writing such a letter, and the fact is, many buyers do write them, and many sellers do read them. I suppose you might say something in a letter that could unintentionally rub the seller the wrong way, but that would be surprising, and certainly the upside to writing one far outweighs the downside. Finally, I know of several buyers chosen in competitive situations, even when they may not have offered the highest price, because of something they wrote.

Here are some tips when drafting a buyer positioning statement:

- First, your agent probably won't help you draft it, nor should they. You know best what you love about the home and your personality will come through better if you write it.
- Steer clear of details about yourself that could reveal your status in a Fair Housing category. Don't talk about your kids, your holiday gatherings, or how the oven will be perfect for baking a big pan of your particular culture's special dessert. (Just say the kitchen is a perfect place to cook large meals.)
- Do talk about the home and neighborhood! Not only will this allow you to steer clear of those Fair Housing categories, people usually like hearing about themselves more than they like hearing about other people. So, talk about how much you love the roses and how you plan on taking care of them. Mention how your dream home always included a soaking tub or wainscoting. Highlight the large basement room and how it will be perfect for movie nights. Share the fact that the home is located on a dead end, and you see them as bringing life to a neighborhood.

True story: I was moved by this exact sentiment in a letter when I sold my personal home. Objectively, the offer was also the best, but I was still touched by the buyers' love of dead ends in the letter.

Bonus: if the sellers haven't depersonalized their home and you see something that you share—maybe you graduated from the same college; maybe you both love Harleys—it doesn't hurt to include that.

- Do talk about how you plan on living there and not just using it as a rental or fix-and-flip project. People love their homes as if they were another family member and the fact that you are the intended occupant can sometimes sway the sellers if a similar competing offer is from an investor.

- While there are several Fair Housing categories, the buyers' financial or employment status is not one of them. Typically, an offer comes with a pre-approval letter from the mortgage lender. If your offer doesn't include one—or proof of funds if you're making an all-cash offer—your agent isn't doing their job. But you may also want to let the seller know you are secure in your employment.

While this doesn't need to go into your letter, a pro-active call from your mortgage lender to the listing agent to assure them that your loan is on track, and all your financial statements and employment have been verified, is probably the most important thing you can do beyond making a strong offer. Having your mortgage lender be pro-active also shows the listing agent that they'll be easy to work with during the transaction since, in most cases, any issues that come up after the inspection will be mortgage related.

- Don't oversell yourself. You still want to get the best deal you can. If something comes up during an inspection, and you want to ask for a price reduction or some other concession from the sellers, you still want to have some negotiating power. Avoid using language like, "I'd do anything to get this home!" or "This is the tenth home we've looked at, and if we don't get it, I don't know what I'll do!"

- Don't include anything negative in the letter like "I really love your home, but what were you thinking painting the walls green?! That will be the first thing we change when we move in!"
- Consider handwriting it (then scanning it, if you're submitting it electronically). The hand-written note is increasingly a thing of a bygone era and will go a long way.
- Keep it short; one-page, typed, or two-pages, handwritten.
- Proofread it. Your attention to detail here will reflect on your attention to detail during the transaction (even if your agent is the one doing most of the work).
- Include your letter in a sealed envelope separate from the rest of the offer (or as a separate attachment, if sending it electronically), so that sellers wanting to refrain from reading it can easily do so.

Finally, remember that while your letter may push your offer over the edge, "highest and best" is almost always the deciding factor, so make your offers objectively strong.

OTHER QUESTIONS BUYERS SHOULD ASK

The sellers will get most of their questions answered just by reviewing the offer and possibly making a counteroffer on a few points. The buyers are at a bit of a loss, though. They only have the information that is provided with the listing, and maybe the property condition report, and some other documentation that's been provided. There are additional questions that buyers should ask that will help them decide whether to make an offer and what kind of offer to make. They may or may not be answered, but it doesn't hurt to ask. The buyers' agent should also be able to answer some of these questions from public records.

- Why are the sellers selling? If you get an overly chatty listing agent, they may let something slip that can help you, the buyers, get a better deal. If you find out that the sellers are being transferred to another city or they're going through a divorce, they're probably pretty motivated to sell as soon as possible and might take a lower offer.

  If you find out that the sellers are moving to a custom-built home and there have been some delays, you might improve your offer by allowing the sellers to stay in the home for a few weeks after it closes.

- How long has the home been on the market? This will be information that is available to your agent, but it's something to keep in mind. The longer it's been on the market, the more likely the sellers are to take a lower offer.

- How much did the sellers pay for the home and how much do they owe on their mortgage? This is another piece of information that is readily available through a public records search. While Idaho is a non-disclosure state and the sales price isn't available to everyone, an agent will be able to look in the MLS and tell you what it sold for and when. Searching the county recorder's website will be able to tell you what mortgages the seller has on the property. You won't be able to get the exact amount the sellers owe, but you'll know what the original mortgage was and you can guess, based on the amount of time that has passed, what is likely still owed. Knowing how much is owed or just how much was originally paid can help your negotiation strategy.

- How many showings have the sellers had? If they've had a lot, you'll probably have some competition. If they've had none, you might be able to come in with an offer under asking price.

- Have the sellers had any offers? Maybe they had an offer that they rejected. This will reveal some of their motivation and what they aren't willing to accept. Maybe they have an offer they're entertaining. They may even tell you the number to beat.

- How old is the roof? Furnace? Hot water heater? These things you'll likely get a pretty good answer to if you do an inspection but knowing that information before you make an offer and pay for an inspection can be valuable. Even if the furnace is working fine at the moment, if it's fifteen years old, you know you'll need to budget for a new one fairly soon.

- What's included in the sale? Typically, only fixtures: things that are attached to the wall like lights, plumbing, and window blinds, are included in a sale. But everything is open for negotiation. If you really love their dining table or if they have a tractor out back, feel free to ask if they'll include it in the sale. They may even throw it in for free and thank you for it because they were stressing out about how to move it.

    On the flip side, there may be something that is a fixture that they're planning on taking with them. One home I sold had a beautiful stained-glass window above the bar. It was of the owner's coat of arms so, naturally, he wanted to take it with him. It was clearly noted, but sometimes things like this won't be noted, so it's best to ask if in doubt. Also, be sure to write into the contract that a certain item will stay or that a certain item needs to be removed.

- What are the sellers' favorite and least favorite parts of the home? The property description can sometimes be very short, and the sellers may not have included some little feature that they love about their home that may be the one thing that tips the scale in favor of you buying it. I sold a home once that had a great view of fireworks on Independence Day. I mentioned this in the marketing material, but not all agents might do the same, so it's a good idea to ask questions.

- Alternatively, that overly chatty agent may let something slip about a downside to the property (the neighbor likes to play drums at 11:30 at night), that will make you think twice about buying it.

© Glasbergen/ glasbergen.com

"Marking your territory is just the first step. If you want the property, you'll also need to put funds into escrow."

CHAPTER 9
NEGOTIATIONS AND CLOSING

PRE-CONTRACT NEGOTIATIONS

You've now received an offer, maybe even a dozen! In a multiple offer situation, some will clearly stand out above the rest. It's time to negotiate.

Your agent should call all the buyers' agents who have put in competitive offers. Actually, your agent should call everyone who's submitted an offer, or even come to see your home and showed any interest in it. You never really know who may be just about to submit an offer or is holding back but can actually submit something much more competitive. Your agent should tell the buyers' agent that they're "very competitive" and ask if they'd like to change their offer at all. This will probably be a price adjustment, but it might be something as simple as asking if they'd be willing to offer a rent-back or put down more earnest money. If you provided offer guidelines, hopefully these sorts of things will have already been addressed.

ACCEPTING/MAKING MULTIPLE OFFERS

You may be wondering if you can accept or make multiple offers. In short, you can't.

If you're the buyer, it is dishonest and illegal to say you're going to buy a home if you can't. If you are going to put an offer on two homes, you better be able to afford both. You might be thinking you can just use your inspection "get-out-of-jail-free card" and back out of the home you like least. I suppose you could, and maybe no one would be the wiser. But if you get caught, you could potentially be sued by the seller. Your agent could also lose their license, which means, if you ask, any good agent is going to say no.

There is one way around that. Every offer you make has an expiration deadline. If you want to make an offer and set it to expire the next day, so you have an opportunity to look at another home that's just come on the market, you can do that. It's actually a great strategy, since even if that expiration date passes and the seller decides to ask if they can accept your offer late, you're always welcome to agree.

As a seller, you *really* can't accept multiple offers. Whereas a buyer could, potentially (but unethically) use several contingencies to get out of a contract. You, as sellers, don't have that option. Once you've sold your home, unless the buyers decide to walk away, you've sold your home. The one way around this is to accept a back-up offer, or even multiple back up offers. This tells the buyers in back up position that, should the first offer fall through, they are now under contract to buy your home at a pre-agreed on price and subject to any pre-agreed upon contingencies. Be sure to fully negotiate this contract, especially if you're the sellers. I spoke to one buyers' agent who helped her clients buy a home for considerably less than they might have because their back up offer wasn't appropriately negotiated by the sellers' agent. Their offer contained an escalation addendum (meaning they agreed to pay a certain amount above the next highest, documented offer), but that escalation addendum was only triggered by the original offer that was accepted. When that original offer went away, there was no competing offer, and her buyers ended up getting the home for the original asking price instead of the escalated price. Good for them. Not so good for the sellers.

Of course, if you don't get multiple offers, you may have to negotiate in a different way. Maybe the one offer you received was less than you'd hoped for. You may just offer to meet in the middle, but remember, the buyers chose the initial bottom end of that spread so meeting in the middle might be lower than you should go. You might also offer to pay some of their closing costs.

Everything is negotiable. You may ask buyers to shorten an inspection period, put more earnest money down, or close earlier.

You should also know your "walk away" point. It can be hard when you have an offer in hand, especially if your home has been on the market longer than you'd hoped, but don't be pressured into accepting something you don't want.

The best time to negotiate these things with both yourself and the buyers is before you accept an offer, because once that offer is accepted, your bargaining power goes way down.

If you're the seller, putting a home back on the market after it has been under contract, even if there was nothing wrong with it, places somewhat of a stigma on it. Other agents will wonder if there's something wrong with it no matter what.

If you're the buyers, hear me now, believe me later, once you're under contract on a home, you've *emotionally* bought that home. Walking away from an inspection that didn't go as well as you'd hoped is going to be a lot harder.

POST-CONTRACT NEGOTIATIONS

Yay! You've bought or sold your home! Well, almost. You're actually under contract now. Until you see that big fat check sitting in your bank account or have the keys in hand, you haven't crossed the finish line. All those contingencies that I've talked about can and do have the potential to make the sale more difficult or cancel it altogether.

A cancelled sale doesn't happen a lot, but it does happen enough that you should be prepared for it and know what to do to prevent it from happening. This is where the post-contract negotiations happen. Of course, as the sellers, the more contingencies you had the buyers waive, the more solid a position you're in.

If your buyers do come back and ask for something, be it for you to fix an item that popped up on an inspection or ask for an extension to closing because their loan officer missed a piece of paperwork, you should strongly consider working it out. If your home goes back on the market, for whatever reason, it will have a stigma attached.

Of course, there are instances when this may be a big win for you, the sellers. If you're in a market strong sellers' market, between the time you accepted that first offer and the time you have to re-list, your home may have gone up in value considerably! If you have a back-up offer in hand, you may not even be losing out on much, if any, money.

COURTESY INSPECTIONS

A word on something called a "courtesy inspection." As sellers, don't allow it. Early on in my career, one of my clients was almost burned by one of these. The buyers had waived the inspection based on the sellers' inspection report, but then asked for a "courtesy inspection" just to see what might need to be fixed from the existing inspection report, and how much it might cost.

My sellers were kind enough to let them conduct this inspection, so the buyers brought in their own inspector. In the real estate world, this type of inspector they hired was known as a deal killer. The guy really had no business being an inspector, even according to the buyers' real estate agent. Thankfully, cooler heads did prevail in the end. (By the way, one very important part of the job of a real estate agent is serving as that cool head in such situations.)

The buyers' agent convinced the nervous buyers that the inspector didn't know what he was talking about, and we moved on. All of this stress could have been avoided by simply and honestly telling the buyers that they were welcome to conduct as thorough of a "courtesy inspection" as they'd like, once the home belonged to them.

While we all have a duty to be honest and forthright about significant issues in our homes, if sellers have had a pre-inspection conducted by a licensed inspector, that is more than enough to show they're not hiding anything. Once under contract, you don't and shouldn't owe the other party anything more than what's in the contract.

Be nice, of course. If buyers want to come in and measure for blinds or ensure the dining table they want to move will fit in the dining room, that's something you should consider allowing. You'll have to let them do a final walk-through a few days before closing anyway.

TITLE AND HOA REVIEW

I covered this a bit earlier, mostly from the sellers' perspective, but I want to cover it again with a little more emphasis on the buyer. The title looks super boring and is filled with a bunch or words that you may not know the meaning of, and like most legal paperwork, probably uses a hundred words when a few will do. But as with most legal paperwork, it's important, so review it. If you don't understand it, call up the title company and ask them to walk you through it.

You don't have to worry much about it being "marketable," i.e., the seller having the legal right to sell it and having all the liens and such paid off. If it isn't marketable, you can't buy it. Of course, if the sellers haven't already cleared any issues, this could be a significant problem for you, if you were planning on moving in on a certain date. Now you either must wait a few more weeks, or worse, have to find another home because the sellers can't actually sell the home period.

The bigger problem as a buyer you need to watch out for pertains to easements, zoning restrictions, HOAs and CC&Rs. If you want to build something somewhere or add a second level, if you simply must store those cars you're working on in the driveway, turn your home into a vacation rental, or have always had a purple and green striped home and always will, you need to make sure all those things are allowed. Once you pass the title contingency period, those aren't reasons for you to back out.

APPRAISAL

The final, typically minor hurdle to overcome during the closing period is the appraisal. The bank really wants to give the seller a loan, so they're going to try to find a way to do that. Since the bank is also going to be owning, 80% or so of the home, they also want to know that what they're buying is worth what they're paying.

Part of this appraisal is ensuring that the home is worth what the buyers are paying for it. To get this information, the appraiser will compare the home to all the other homes in the area that have recently sold and are similar. It's much more detailed than the CMA your agent did, but it's the same general idea. The appraiser will also verify some things about the home. They'll probably do an outside measurement to get a general idea of the square footage. They'll also look for some key health and safety items. For instance, is there any evidence of flooding? Does the roof appear to have at least five years left of useful life? Does it have an electrical panel that hasn't been recalled? Are smoke detectors in every bedroom and on every floor?

When obtaining a conventional loan, these appraisals, while somewhat thorough, are typically not very stringent. If the buyer is putting enough down or you're just lucky, the appraiser may just do a "drive-by" appraisal, which means exactly what is sounds like. They may even do a "drive-by" via their computer and just look at existing records on the home.

If the buyer has FHA, VA, or some other government backed loan, the appraiser will be a bit more stringent. An FHA appraisal basically involves a more thorough look at the property and some additional "health and safety" issues that may be called out.

If, for some reason, the home doesn't pass appraisal, it's still probably worth addressing the issues rather than going back on the market. You may have to do some minor repairs (hopefully they're minor), or you may have to renegotiate the price. As the sellers, know that if your home didn't appraise for value, unless it's a really strong sellers' market, it's a good idea to give a little on the price, if necessary. If it didn't appraise the first time, it probably won't appraise the second time. If it was an FHA appraisal, that stays on record for six months, so it definitely won't appraise the second time for all other FHA buyers.

THE FINAL WALK-THROUGH

You are so close to the finish line. Everything has been approved, and all that's left to do is a final verification of the buyers' financials and the signing. But before that happens, the buyers will definitely want to do a walk-through of the property a day or two before closing.

I find most sellers are decent folks who will want to turn over their homes to the new buyers in the best condition possible. Unfortunately, some will not. While sellers don't have the obligation to turn over their home in the best condition possible, they do have an obligation to turn it over in the condition it was in when the buyers first viewed it. They also have an obligation to leave it empty and clean (unless agreed upon otherwise) and make any repairs specified in the contract.

The final walk-through will ensure that everything you asked to be fixed is fixed and the home is, more or less, clean. I say "more or less" because everyone's definition of clean is different. You might get lucky and move into a home that looks like it belongs in a cleaning products ad. But do understand, most sellers are usually frantically trying to clean up until the last minute and probably won't be getting down on their hands and knees with a toothbrush. As long as it's reasonably clean, you should proceed to closing since you probably don't want to hold up your own move over something so minor. You're also not going to be able to back out of the contract because the home is dirty or there are a bunch of small nail holes left in the wall from the pictures that had been hanging there.

If the home is not in a suitable condition though, if there is significant trash all over the place or they made a big hole in the wall while moving furniture, require that it be cleaned up before agreeing to sign.

The final walk-through applies to the outside as well as the inside. An agent told me a story about some clients who bought a home from someone who owned a dog that used the backyard for his daily business and the owners never cleaned up after the dog. This agent was smart and noted in the contract that all of that mess would need to be picked up.

ESCROW, SIGNING, AND CLOSING

You've probably heard the word "escrow" thrown around a few times and wonder what it is. Whether you're the buyers or sellers, this is probably the biggest transaction of your life. While it would be nice to do things on a smile and a handshake, handing over that amount of money in exchange for a piece of paper that confirms you own a chunk of land and the improvements on it, is probably not the best idea. So, you'll want to go through a neutral, third-party. That's escrow. Escrow will hold on to your earnest money and then act as a go-between for the transfer of the final payment directly from you or from the bank where you're getting your mortgage. They'll also handle the transfer and recording of the title with the county and ensure any taxes, fees, and final utility bills attached to the property are paid. What if the sellers didn't pick up all the little presents their dog left in the backyard? Escrow will hold back funds and refuse to close until that requirement is met too. They'll also coordinate the final signing appointment for buyers and sellers.

The final step is signing over title and, if you're the buyers, signing some final loan documents. You should have already reviewed this paperwork and your eyes might be bleeding at this point, but make sure to review it once again. If there are any questions, call your mortgage broker, real estate agent, or the escrow officer.

While all the paperwork is important, the most common place that mistakes are discovered are on the HUD statement. This is a debit and credit sheet with all the sellers' costs and credits on one side and all the buyers' costs and credits on the other. This is where you'll see any government taxes and fees that are being paid at closing as well as things like your agent's compensation.

Typically, all this signing will be done at the escrow company's office. This is preferable, since the escrow officer will be right there to walk you through everything and answer any questions. You're welcome to invite your real estate agent and mortgage broker to this signing as well.

If you're unable to go to the escrow office, the escrow office can usually send a mobile notary to your home. Be aware that this mobile notary doesn't know the particulars of your contract or mortgage though, so they won't be able to answer any specific question. And in case you were wondering, a mobile notary can meet you almost anywhere. I had another agent tell me about how she had to arrange for a mobile notary to meet a seller at the U.S. Embassy in Nigeria! So, don't fret if the closing of your sale ends up happening the same day that you are on vacation in Hawaii. The other alternative to signing remotely is to sign a day or two earlier, if possible. If all the paperwork is ready, this should not be an issue.

And that's it. Congratulations, you've bought a home! The sellers will probably have delivered the keys to their real estate agent, who will then deliver them to yours, who will deliver them to you.

"I opened my checkbook. Then I opened it again.
Then I opened it again. Then I opened it again.
So how come the bank called it a 'closing'?"

CHAPTER 10
MOVING TO YOUR NEW HOME!

It's now time to move into your new home. If you're hiring a professional moving service, all of this should be arranged from the start, since moving companies can be scheduled out a few weeks. They'll send someone to your home who will give you an idea of how much it will cost to move everything. You may even want to hire them to pack your things. This, of course, can be pricey, but it may be worth it. After all, for most people who've left the college days of futons and milk crate storage behind, you probably have far more stuff than you realize.

Moving companies generally charge by weight, so if you want to find some big cost savings, you may want to pack up those barbells and the collected works of Shakespeare and transport them separately. Moving away is also a great time to purge some of the items you haven't touched in years. The other reason all this should be addressed before you list your house is the less stuff you have in your home before listing, the larger and neater it will look.

WELCOME TO YOUR NEW HOME!
NOW WHAT?

The moving van is parked outside, and the movers are transporting all your worldly possessions into your new home. What now? You'll probably want to find the toilet paper and then head out to the closest restaurant, since you're exhausted, and all the stuff needed to cook dinner was somehow packed away in the box labeled "OLD FAMILY PHOTOS." But, once that is done, there are some important things you'll need to take care of ASAP.

• **Homeowner's Tax Exemption**—In Idaho (and several other states, although not all), we operate under the Homestead Act. I won't go into the fascinating history of the Homestead Act, but the area that's most important to you, the new homeowners, is the tax exemption. If the home you just bought is your primary residence, you're entitled to a partial exemption on your property taxes. Specifically, you're entitled to deduct up to half your property's (improvements and up to one acre) value up to $125,000. This means that if you own a home on a 1/4 acre that's valued by the assessor at $400,000, you only pay taxes on $275,000. (If you own more than an acre and/or your property is valued at under $200,000, you'll be exempted from half the value of the home and one of the acres.)

• **Utilities**—Hopefully, your escrow company made sure that all the old owners' utility obligations were paid at closing, but you'll still need to call all your local utility providers to initiate new service under your name. Most of these can be contacted before you actually move, to insure there's no interruption in service. Some utilities, like internet and cable, sometimes must send someone out, so an appointment

is required, and that should be booked well ahead of time. Here's a list of the common utilities:
- Water
- Sewer
- Garbage
- Gas/Electricity
- Internet/Telephone
- Cable/Satellite

- **Postal Service**—Go to USPS.com and fill out a change of address form. You'll also want to contact everyone who regularly sends you mail to let them know your new address as the Postal Service will typically only forward first-class mail for one year.
- **Driver's License, Voter Registration, Library**— Contact the DMV to update your address on your driver's license and vehicle registration. Also, remember to update your voter registration with your county election's office or secretary of state, and get a new library card if you now live in a new library district.
- **Keys & Locks**—You received keys to your home upon closing. I'm sure the people you purchased the home from are completely honorable, but you never know how many extra keys may be floating around out there. It's always best to change the locks and any digital codes used to access the home, like the garage door opener. Consider upgrading to a "smart" lock at this time. They don't cost much more than an key lock and will come in handy if you ever have to open the door remotely.
- **Your Recorded Deed**—You can expect to receive an original copy of your deed from your county recorder's office within 4-6 weeks after closing. Keep this in a safe and secure place.
- **Loan Payments**—unless you paid all cash for your new home, you'll likely be making monthly payments

to your lender. Make note of the due date of your payments in case you don't get a reminder. You may want to set up an auto-payment. Also, you may want to pay on a bi-weekly schedule instead of a monthly schedule. You'll hardly notice the difference, but the extra payment you end up making each year does add up to considerable savings over the course of your loan. You may also receive notice that your loan was sold to another company anywhere from a few months to a year after closing. For your protection, make sure to contact your current lender before sending in payment to any new companies.

- **Property Taxes & Homeowner's Insurance**—If you have a loan, taxes and homeowner's insurance are paid through an escrow account held by your mortgage company. They will likely take out a percentage of what is owed each month and then pay these bills when they come due. Occasionally, if your homeowner's insurance or property taxes go up, you may have to make an extra payment to your escrow account to ensure it has enough money. At closing, a percentage of upcoming taxes as well as your homeowner's insurance payment should have also been taken out by escrow as part of your closing costs. However, it is the responsibility of the homeowners to ensure taxes and insurance are paid on time and in full, so confirm with your lender or county assessor that your taxes are being paid and when the due date is.
- **Getting Social & Making New Friends**—You're moving to a new area. You'll probably want to get plugged in with a new group of friends. Here are some great ideas to do this.
    - Knock on your neighbors' doors. Hopefully some will knock on yours and welcome you to the neighborhood, but don't wait. Of course, not all of them will end up being your new best

friends. Some may not even be particularly neighborly. You may be surprised by how many will become a part of your social circle and support structure, though. If knocking on a door is a little outside your comfort zone, just get out and take walks through the neighborhood or go to the local park.

- Join a club or organization. This may be a faith community, a service organization like Rotary or Kiwanis, a sports league or gym, or a book club.
- Read the local newspaper. It probably lists lots of community events where you can get out and meet people.
- Volunteer. Of course, this is an integral part of most faith communities and service organizations, but you don't have to be part of a larger group to volunteer. Whether it's donating blood or joining in a local neighborhood cleanup, it doesn't even need to be a big commitment and it's a great way to meet people who share your passion.
- Take a class. This doesn't have to be a semester long slog at the local university. Consider something that lasts just a few weeks or even meets just once, like a cooking class or paint your own pottery night. Who knows who you might end up sitting next to?
- Go online. I don't mean go on Facebook or Instagram. Those may be great and an important way to keep in touch with your old friends, but for most people, a true sense of community has to have some literal face-to-face interaction. This can start online though. Meetup is a great way to find clubs that are meeting in your area. Eventbrite also has

events happening in your local area. Of course, there might be some good events advertised on Facebook as well. Just remember, you're probably not going to gain any meaningful relationships by staring at your phone or computer screen all day.

CHAPTER 11
THINGS TO CONSIDER WHEN HIRING A REAL ESTATE AGENT

By now, you have a good idea of all the things that go into buying and selling a home. If you feel prepared to take on the task alone, good for you! Seriously! While it can be time-consuming, complicated, and come with many risks, there are plenty of people who've decided to list their homes without an agent and have been pleased with the results.

Furthermore, saving tens of thousands of dollars in listing fees might be worth the extra work and risk. I'll go even further and say that, if you've already found a buyer, especially if they are a trusted friend of family member, and you've all agreed on the price and process, you're probably okay not hiring an agent, although you may want to pay a real estate attorney a nominal fee to review the contract.

For those of you who have read through this book and found the process too daunting, don't feel alone. According to the National Association of Realtors, 92% of sellers hire an agent. What's more, the average home listed with an agent sells for 11% more than one listed For Sale By Owner (FSBO). Keep in mind, too, that when someone lists on their own, they will probably still end up paying a buyers' agent's compensation. The savings just aren't there, and you'll have all that extra work to do. So, for those of you who have decided to hire a real estate agent, here are some things to consider.

WHAT A GOOD AGENT WON'T DO

Back when I sold radio advertising, there was a woman in my office who'd often, without a hint of irony, say, "That's not my job." Needless to say, she didn't last long. I'm of the opinion that if my client needs something, it *is* my job, and if I don't know how or I'm not legally authorized to do said job, I'd better find someone who is. Of course, there are some things a real estate agent can't legally do.

- Like George Washington, real estate agents cannot tell a lie. This also pertains to withholding material facts. As an example, if you're the seller, and you tell me your basement flooded, you must disclose that on your Property Condition Disclosure. If you choose not to, I will not be representing you. If you're a buyer and you don't qualify for the price of the home you're looking at, I can't tell the sellers that you do, even if you *know* you have the winning lottery ticket in your wallet.
- In that same vein, real estate agents can't help you commit mortgage fraud. If you're planning on arranging with the sellers to buy their home at an inflated price, then have them give you money back so that your mortgage is covering something other than your home (like a trip to Hawaii, a new boat, or even planned upgrades or repairs to your new home), that's mortgage fraud. This is such a serious offense that there's actually an FBI warning included in all the loan paperwork you'll sign. If you're caught committing mortgage fraud, you may go to prison.

- Real estate agents can't give you legal advice they are not licensed to give. If a transaction runs into a major legal issue, I'm going to tell you to consult an attorney. If a property has a maintenance or title issue, I'm going to refer you to an inspector or a title officer.
- While there may be gray areas that are technically legal, if I consider it unethical, I will not do it. In general, if you have the attitude of winning at all costs or sticking it to the other party in the transaction, I'm not the agent for you. I believe in a win-win situation in almost all cases. This means, while I will represent my clients fully and find the best deal for them alone, if it comes down to it, I'm not going to help my clients punish the other party or suck every last drop of blood out of them.
- I won't act as your personal tour guide or chauffeur. I'm more than happy to drive you around and show you homes. I've even driven hundreds of miles in a day to do so. But I do need to know this is a two-way street. If I get the impression that you're just using me to look at homes you have no intention of buying, I'm not the right agent for you.

WHAT A GOOD REAL ESTATE AGENT WILL DO

This book is mostly about all the things any decent real estate agents should do, but there are a few other things that aren't under my general job description that I am happy to take on.

- If you're in a scheduling bind, have gone on vacation, or already moved out of the area in which you're selling, there's quite a bit I'm willing to do. If you need your trash cans taken out and brought back in, let me know. If you need me to meet a contractor or home cleaner, I view this as an integral part of my job. If you need me to meet the moving van, I'm your man. In fact, if it's a small move, and it doesn't make sense to hire a moving company, I've even been known to rent a U-Haul and load up the few pieces of furniture you may need to transport to your new home.

- I'm willing to do the minor repairs and cleaning I'm qualified to do. If a light bulb burns out, I'll replace it. If your driveway needs pressure washing, as long as it's not a mile long, I'll do it.
- I'll be your shoulder to cry on. Buying or selling a home can be stressful. I'm not a licensed therapist by any means, but if you need to vent about something, even if it's not necessarily related to the home buying process, feel free to share your stresses with me.

NOT ALL AGENTS ARE EQUAL

There are some people in my industry who will bad mouth what they sometimes pejoratively refer to as *discount* brokers behind their backs (and maybe to their faces). I'm not one of them. First of all, I don't believe in building myself up by tearing other people down. Furthermore, I've done transactions with so-called discount agents who have been on the ball every step of the way and were a joy to work with. I've also done business with some agents who worked for premier brokerages and was shocked by how little they knew about how to do their jobs.

For this reason, I use the word *discount*, not as a disapproval, but as a better description. There might be full-service agents charging full-service rates and giving you limited, or even poor service, and there might be limited-service agents who go above and beyond and all at a reduced rate. (On a side note, experience isn't always the barometer it should be, either. The two transactions I've had the most difficulty with were with agents who'd been in the business for quite some time, and they'd done hundreds of transactions. Yet, they were downright dishonest in one case, and had apparently forgotten some very basic things in another.)

What should you be considering when hiring an agent?

- After I just said experience isn't always the barometer it should be, I will tell you that it often is. Like anything, the more someone does it, the better they will get. This is partly because practice makes perfect, as they say, but also, because of how unique each transaction can be. The more transactions an agent does, the more situations they will be familiar with. That's not to say you shouldn't hire a brand-new agent doing their first deal. Just make sure they are working alongside a good mentor who will be reviewing everything they do. (You might even suggest that the rookie agent co-list your home with their mentor or someone else with more experience in their office. Most experienced agents will be happy to do so. Believe it or not, this business isn't the cutthroat atmosphere you may have seen in movies.)

- How available is your agent? This is definitely one of the most important things. Deals can come down to a matter of hours. If your agent spends too much time on the golf course, at another job, or just has so many clients they can't devote the time necessary to your transaction, you might want to find someone else.

    If they're a friend of yours, and you'd still like to give them the business, consider asking them to refer you to someone else. That might be a delicate conversation, but nonetheless, they'll get a referral fee for doing so and they might thank you for it. They might have been wondering how they could refer you to someone else without offending *you*!

On the flip side, do realize that while a good agent works evenings and weekends, real estate agents do have lives and families and other clients. So, there may be times when they can't get right back to you. The best agents will tell you when they're not available and how long it will typically take to get back to you. They will also have back-up, another agent in their office who they can get to cover for them if they're unavailable.

- How professional is your agent? This might be offensive to those folks who have a system to that messy desk or the office they carry around in the trunk of their car, but there are hundreds of small steps to a real estate transaction. Many of them have ironclad deadlines and pieces of paper that go along with them. It's said that a messy desk is the sign of genius. That may be the case, but I'm not sure I would have wanted Albert Einstein handling the details of my real estate transaction. After all, how much more big picture can you get than the Theory of Relativity?

- Along those lines, because this is a professional industry and agents are judged by other agents based on their professionalism, your agent should carry themselves in a professional manner. If you're buying a beach home in The Bahamas, flip-flops and cut offs might be considered the dress of the day, but even if you don't care, some agents will look somewhat askance at agents who aren't dressed properly or don't carry themselves professionally. True story: Wendy Lister, the "Queen of Northwest Real Estate" (more about her in the resume section near the end of the book) didn't know me from Adam the first time I met her, but she invited me to come work with her the next day because, as she said, I dressed and spoke professionally when we met. True story #2: On a transaction where I represented the buyer, when the deal had closed and the listing agent and I were celebrating, she told me one of the reasons her client picked our offer was that I'd represented myself in a professional manner, and he felt that was a good sign that the transaction would go smoothly.

- What brokerage is your agent affiliated with? When I first started in this business, I was under the impression that all brokerages were essentially the same, and things really came down to the individual agent. While things certainly do come down to the individual agent and great brokerages can have lousy agents and lousy brokerages can have great agents, not all brokerages are created equal.

  I quickly realized that after I had the opportunity to experience working for two different brokerages and comparing them. A more professional brokerage typically has more training opportunities for its agents, as well as transaction support and marketing. It will also have a lot of institutional knowledge, meaning that there are several people I can consult if I need a second opinion or help with a particularly difficult situation.

  It also might mean it's more professional. Just as agents will judge one another based on how they individually represent themselves, they will also judge agents, rightly or wrongly, based on which brokerage they work for. There are certain brokerages that have a less than stellar reputation.

"This little pig built his house from straw,
but it sold for $599,000. That's the
real estate agent we should use!"

CLOSING

I want to thank you for taking the time to read this book. Hopefully, it was worth it, and you've learned some things that will help you with the purchase or sale of your home. If you'd like to know more about me and why I am a real estate agent, please read the Afterward. Please visit my website as well, where I post articles that go more in depth on topics covered in this book or even cover completely new topics. I also share articles I've enjoyed related to the world of real estate.

With that, I wish you the best of luck with your purchase or sale and with the next chapter of your life in your new home. And, as George and Mary Bailey said in *It's a Wonderful Life,* may you have

"Bread, that this home may never know hunger.
Salt, that life may always have flavor.
And wine, that joy and prosperity may reign forever!"

Mark Griswold
www.RefugePropertiesNorthIdaho.com

AFTERWORD

IT'S A WONDERFUL LIFE!
WHY I'M A REAL ESTATE AGENT

Most real estate agents will tell you this business isn't about homes, it's about people, and because it's about people, you should know who the information in this book is coming from and who you might be hiring to help you buy or sell your home. (I'm also a people person and believe the more we know about each other, the friendlier we'll be. And we could definitely use more friendliness in this world!)

***

I've been in sales most of my adult life. In fact, one might say I've been in sales my entire life. And so have you! All life is sales since sales is nothing more than doing something to elicit a response.

When my son brings a granola bar over, looks at me with puppy dog eyes, and in the cute way only he can, asks me to open it for him, he is selling me on the idea of needing the granola bar. Maybe in twenty years, he'll be opening doors instead of granola bars; doors to new homeownership!

Like my son, I'm sure I sold my parents on the idea of a cookie or a new set of LEGOs. I distinctly remember my first lemonade stand and selling candy bars door to door for a school fundraiser. Once I became a grownup, I continued in sales professionally. Prior to selling real estate, I sold everything from cruise vacations to corkscrews. The latest thing I sold before homes was radio advertising, so you might say I went from selling air to selling dirt! Except, I don't actually sell dirt.

There's an old saying, "People don't buy a drill, they buy lots of little holes." But even that isn't true. They're buying a hole in the wall so they can hang a picture that will, in turn, bring them joy. People buy feelings.

So, what I sell is a sense of security in the physical sense, a place to hold belongings and sleep safely at night. In an abstract sense, I sell a place to plan for the future and look forward to memories yet to come, as well as the financial sense. According to the Federal Reserve's 2020 *Survey of Consumer Finances*, homeowners had a median net worth more than 40 times greater than that of renters.

To some extent, people also buy homes out of pride. This is not necessarily a bad thing, as long as their pride doesn't get the better of them and turn into an envious race to "keep up with the Joneses." Pride of homeownership leads to an emotional investment in the community, since people typically take better care of something they own versus something they are borrowing (or in this case, renting.) According to a 2016 Habitat for Humanity study, this emotional investment translates into safer communities, increased health and graduation rates, decreased behavioral problems in children, and even a pathway out of poverty.

This opportunity to help people build wealth, escape poverty, and make our communities safer; this opportunity to give people The American Dream and the pride and sense of security that goes along with it, is what I love about being a real estate agent.

My favorite movie of all time is *It's A Wonderful Life*. There are so many great lessons in it: the importance of family, friends, and faith; delayed gratification; doing the right thing even when it's difficult; even the importance of having a good throwing arm! I tear up every time I watch it and have for many years. But it wasn't until

I re-watched it after becoming a real estate agent that George Bailey's profession took on new meaning.

George, after all, is in the real estate business. And in the best way! He helps renters in Potter's slums become homeowners in Bailey Park. If you haven't watched the movie in a while, go back and do so. There are many great lessons to be learned from it. But regarding real estate, pay attention to the scene where George and Mary welcome Mr. Martini and his family to their new home. That scene was an inspiration, quite literally, for me and, if you do end up buying a home from me, you'll receive that same welcome, complete with "bread, that [your] home may never know hunger; salt, that life may have flavor; and wine, that joy and prosperity may reign forever!"

In 2020, this passion to help people find the security and pride of homeownership took on a whole new dimension. That year, many of our cities were in crisis with crime at levels not seen in generations. Many police forces were vilified because of the poor actions of a very small number of individual officers. Blocks and blocks were literally being taken over and buildings burned. On top of this, businesses were shuttered by force, leading to a level of permanent closure not seen in a lifetime, if ever. And while schools did reopen, the time they were closed forced many parents to stay home instead of going to a job that might have existed, contributing to a horrible downward cycle of economic ruin that was only staved off by record levels of government spending, a bill that will eventually come due.

People can disagree on why all this has occurred and whether the actions taking place are a good thing or not. But the fact is, we saw a level of migration within this nation that hadn't occurred in a hundred years or more. Many of these migrants left big cities with high crime rates for more rural areas with less crime. They left states that were in lockdown or instituting other measures many see as draconian for states with more freedom.

My family and I are part of this story. Thankfully, my wife's job allows her to work from home indefinitely. Because of the rising crime and rioting in the Seattle area, and the inability of our three children to attend school, we packed up and moved to Coeur d'Alene, Idaho. It was one of the fastest growing cities in our nation in the fastest growing state.

This whole new chapter in my life and our nation's history, one that will hopefully have a happy ending someday, not only led us to flee the Seattle area, but has increased my passion for helping others do the same, to flee the madness and turmoil of big cities for a place where a slower pace of life still exists, the neighbors are more neighborly, and the freedom of the individual and the family is still respected.

So, that's a bit about me and why I am a real estate agent. But all the passion in the world without the proper knowledge can be a dangerous thing so, in the next section, I'll go over why I'm not only a passionate real estate agent, but a knowledgeable one as well.

"I used to sell mud pies, but I can charge more if I call it real estate."

REAL ESTATE RÉSUMÉ

I've been a real estate agent the Coeur d'Alene area since 2020. Prior to that, I practiced in the Seattle area since being licensed in 2017. For some of those years in Seattle, I was blessed to have worked with a wonderful woman named Wendy Lister. When Wendy passed away after a many-decades-long and distinguished career as a real estate agent, she was lauded in the local press with headlines that proclaimed her the "Queen of Northwest Real Estate" and similar monikers.

During her career, she was responsible for many changes and improvements to the real estate industry in Washington state and probably nationwide. She specialized in luxury real estate and sold at least a few of the "most expensive estates ever sold" in Washington state, some to people you would clearly recognize. Best of all, Wendy wasn't just an industry leader, she was also one of the kindest people I've ever met. I'm blessed to have been able to call her a mentor for the too-short time I knew her. I'd like to think some of her experience, as well as her kind demeanor, rubbed off on me.

Beyond my experience as a licensed real estate agent, I've also overseen the remodel of homes and have owned investment properties. While this doesn't directly pertain to most buyers who are only looking for a primary residence, it is, nonetheless, helpful and informative to most transactions I guide in one way or another.

Finally, I've taken literally hundreds of hours of classes; so many, in fact, I won't bore you with the long list. Some highlights though, that also earned me the privilege of putting a bunch of letters after my name:

I am an **Accredited Buyers Representative (ABR)** and a **Seller Representative Specialist (SRS)**. This means I have served as the buyers' and sellers' agent on the requisite number of homes and have gone through several hours of classes that went over how best to represent my clients.

Most of what I learned in these class I had already learned as part of the actual selling process, but the book learning did help underscore some key strategies and scenarios. If nothing else, it serves as an objective measure that I know what I'm doing.

I am a **Master Certified Negotiation Expert (MCNE)**. This means I've gone through several hours of classes on negotiation techniques. I'm grateful to have many of the tools and tactics I learned through these classes (as well as in the real world, both as a real estate agent and in general), because deals can sometimes fall apart when the wrong negotiation strategy (or no strategy at all) is employed. There are many reasons to hire real estate agents, but one of the most important may be their ability to get the deal done and on the most favorable terms to their clients. I've been part of transactions where, thankfully, the negotiation skills I've learned and honed over time have saved or made my clients tens of thousands of dollars or saved the deal itself.

I am a **Certified Real Estate Analyst (CREA)**. This is especially useful if you're looking for an income producing property, but even if you're just looking for your primary residence, it shouldn't be solely about how much you love the neighborhood and the layout of the home, although those things are probably the most important. A home is always an investment, or at least it should be. Only you can know if you love the home you're looking at and want to make it yours. By analyzing the numbers associated with the home and its surrounding market though, I can give you an idea of how reasonable a financial investment it is.

While I don't get any letters next to my name for other classes I've taken, in many ways I've found several of them even more useful. Perhaps the most valuable have been the classes related to inspections and major issues that can be present in a home. Of course, I'm not a licensed inspector and I strongly encourage all my clients to get an inspection done before buying a home.

Knowing what things to look out for is very valuable in assessing properties both in terms of finding some red flags, as well as knowing about things that might appear scary, but are probably not as bad as they seem, yet are worth hiring an inspector to look into it further.

I've also taken several classes and seminars on real estate law. I take at least one of these per year. Topics include zoning, housing affordability, real estate development, and forms. There are dozens and dozens of forms to fill out, and they too, sometimes change year to year. Going over them in detail is important.), I've also taken classes on marketing, finance and credit, loan programs, title, escrow, wire fraud, insurance, home warranties, water rights, property and other types of taxes, easements, liens and encumbrances, remodeling, interior design, moving (yes, there was even a class on that!), and much more.

All of these classes and those I will continue to take, along with countless articles related to real estate that I read regularly, help me provide a high level of expertise and service to my clients. Thankfully, I'm also a bit of a real estate nerd, so I've enjoyed most of them. I surprised even myself one time when I actually uttered the words, without a hint of irony, "That class on zoning was fascinating!"

That's me in a nutshell. Thanks again for reading my book, and I look forward to helping you with your real estate needs in the future.

"I am required by law to inform you that there are skeletons in the closet and a monster living under one of the beds. But we anticipate that they will be vacating with the current occupants."

TYPES OF SERVICE PROVIDERS

Here's a list of all the professionals who help me do my job or help you once you've moved into your new home.

appraiser—someone hired by the bank who makes sure that the price you're paying is reasonable from their perspective, and that the home is what it is reported to be.

contractor (plumber, electrician, roofer, HVAC specialist, painter, etc.)—people who can come in and fix anything that's broken or not to your liking.

escrow officer—someone who holds on to money that's in transition between buyer and seller and who ensures that all the necessary paperwork is being submitted on time and the transaction process is running smoothly. Sometimes called a "closing agent".

home inspector—someone who inspects the physical aspects of your home to make sure what you think you're buying is what you're actually buying. In addition to general home inspectors, you may need to hire inspectors who specialize in things like wells, septic systems, roofs, structural engineering, and more.

landscaper—someone who comes in and makes the outside of your home look like it belongs on HGTV.

mortgage lender—someone who helps you get money to buy your home.
mover—someone who will save you the headache and backache of having to pack up all your furniture and move it to your new home.

photographer—someone who knows how to capture what the stager did in such a way that it looks like it belongs on HGTV for those who aren't seeing it in person.

recorder—a public official who keeps records of transactions that affect real property in the area. Also called a County Clerk.

stager—someone who comes in and makes the inside of your home look like it belongs in a magazine or on TV so it will attract more potential buyers.

title officer—someone who researches title to make sure what you think you're buying, in the legal sense, is what you're actually buying.

GLOSSARY

This is, by no means, an exhaustive list of terms used in real estate, but does cover most of the often-used terms.

absorption rate—the rate at which available homes are sold in a specific market during a given time period.

appraisal—a professional analysis used to estimate the value of the property.

assessed value—the value placed on the property by, typically, the county assessor, for taxing purposes.

buyer positioning statement (aka buyer love letter)—a letter written from the buyers to the sellers stating reasons they want the home and why the sellers should pick them.

CC&Rs—Covenants, Conditions & Restrictions are limits and rules placed on a group of homes or condominium complex by a builder, developer, neighborhood, or homeowners' association.

closing costs—the upfront fees charged in connection with a real estate transaction. These can include loan origination fees, title examination, escrow fees, title insurance, survey fees, and prepaid items such as taxes and homeowners' insurance.

closing date—the date on which the sale of the property will be complete and recorded with the county.
closing period—the time from when mutual acceptance is reached between the buyer and seller and the closing date.

CMA—a Comparative Market Analysis is an analysis of other properties similar to the subject property that have recently sold. A CMA is a common way of determining the listing price of a home. The other properties are sometimes referred to as "comps."

condominium—a legal term that applies to properties where a portion (like an individual unit) is owned by one entity (person or persons, corporation, partnership) and the rest the property (common areas) is owned by all the owners in common. Condominiums don't have to be single buildings. Something that looks like a neighborhood of houses could also legally be a condominium.

contingency—a condition that must be met before a contract is legally binding.

conventional mortgage—a mortgage that is not insured or guaranteed by a federal government agency like the FHA, USDA, or VA. It is, however, backed by Fannie Mae, so has a limit on what can be loaned. Loans above that amount are classified as "Jumbo Loans."

curb appeal—the visual attractiveness of a property when initially seen by a potential buyer who is standing at the curb.

deed—the legal document transferring ownership or title to a property.

down payment—a portion of the price of a home, typically 3%-20%, not borrowed, and paid upfront in cash.

earnest money—a deposit to show that a buyer is committed to buying a home. This will only be refunded if one of the contingencies in the contract is not met.

easement—a right to use or access land (or air above or dirt below the land in some cases) owned by another.

encroachment—the intrusion onto another's property, sometimes without a legal right.

encumbrance—any claim on a property, such as a lien.

equity—the value in a home above the total amount of liens against it.

escalation notice or addendum—a notice or addendum to an offer that tells the seller that the buyer will beat the next highest offer by a certain amount up to a certain amount.

escrow—an item of value, such as money or documents, deposited with a third party to be delivered upon fulfillment of a condition.

excise tax—a tax paid by the seller of a property when that property is sold. Idaho is one of fourteen states that does not have a Real Estate Excise Tax. Washington has one of the highest in the nation.

FIRPTA—Foreign Investment in Real Property Tax Act. A law that imposes capital gains tax on foreign persons selling U.S. real estate.

FHA—the Federal Housing Authority. A federal agency that insures mortgages made by private lenders.

foreclosure—legal action that ends all ownership rights to a home when the owner fails to make mortgage, tax, or other lien payments.

HOA—Homeowners Association. An organization of homeowners whose purpose is to ensure the maintenance of community facilities and enforcement of CC&Rs (see above).

home warranty—a policy that covers certain home repairs and fixtures.

homeowner's exemption—a certain percentage of value of a property that is exempted from taxation. Idaho has a homeowner's exemption. Washington does not.

HUD-1 statement—a final listing of closing costs on a mortgage transaction.

keybox—a box, typically accessed with an electronic key held by a real estate agent, that holds the physical key to a property.

legal description—how a property is described for legal purposes. This is typically a reference to a description recorded with the county. For properties not recorded with the county, other methods, like metes-and-bounds are used.

lien—a claim or charge on property for payment of a debt. A mortgage is a type of lien.

MLS—Multiple Listing Service. A database of most of the properties being sold in an area.

mortgage—a loan using your home as collateral.

mutual acceptance—the point at which the buyer and seller reach agreement, in writing, on the purchase and sales agreement.

net proceeds—the amount a seller gets from the sale of their house after all mortgages, liens, agent compensation, and any other fees associated with the sale are paid.

notary public—a person who has the authority to act as an official witness when legal documents are signed.

PITI—Principle, Interest, Taxes, and Insurance. The four primary components of a monthly mortgage payment. The mortgage company will pay your taxes and homeowners insurance on your behalf.

possession date—the date on which a buyer is allowed to move into the home. This is usually the same day as closing but could be before or after if a rental agreement is in place.

pre-approval—when a lender indicates to prospective buyers how much they are eligible to borrow. This typically includes a review of credit history and income and employment verification.

pre-inspection—having a licensed inspector inspect a home for any flaws before it is listed. It may also be when a prospective buyer has an inspection conducted before submitting an offer.

pre-qualification—a preliminary assessment by a lender of the amount they will lend to a prospective buyer. This does not include a review of credit, income, or employment so isn't really worth the paper it's printed on.

Private Mortgage Insurance (PMI)—Insurance on a conventional loan that protects the lender from loss in the event that the borrower defaults. This is typically owed until the loan is paid down below 80% of the value of the home.

Property Condition Report—a real estate form filled out by the seller indicating certain material facts about the property, including if systems like heating, plumbing, and electrical are working or have been repaired, and if there has ever been flooding, pest infestation, or roof damage, amongst other things. Called a Seller Disclosure Statement in Washington.

property taxes—yearly taxes owed on a property. These are often paid semi-annually and fund things like schools, parks, and fire departments.

Purchase-and-Sales Agreement (PSA)—the main contract in a real estate transaction.

recording—the filing of a lien or other legal document into the public record.

rent-back—when the buyer agrees to rent back to the seller the home that's just been purchased. This can typically be done up to 60 days without having to get a non-owner-occupied loan.

reverse offer—when the seller makes an offer to a prospective buyer to purchase the home.

seller financing—when the seller provides the financing for the buyers' purchase of the property.

short sale—when a property is sold for less than what is owed on the mortgage.

title—the right to a property. Proof of ownership of land.

title insurance—insurance that protects owners and lenders against problems with the title.

USDA loan—a zero down, low interest mortgage guaranteed by the U.S. Department of Agriculture. Only available on properties in rural areas as defined by the USDA.

VA loan—a zero down, low interest mortgage guaranteed by the U.S. Department of Veterans Affairs and available to veterans or active-duty members of the military.

walk-through—a common clause in a sales contract allowing the buyers to examine the property immediately (typically 1-3 days) before closing.

zoning—local laws or regulations that govern how a property can and cannot be used in a certain area.

"It's the perfect home for a couple who can't decide what they want. It's a victorian split-level colonial ranch mobile cabin!"

CHECKLISTS

SELLING PROCESS

Pre-listing
- Research property
    - Market history and last listed date
    - Annual taxes
    - Zoning
    - HOA bylaws and CC&Rs
    - Surveys, easements, and encumbrances
    - Liens
    - Info about neighborhood (schools, amenities)
- CMA/pricing your home
    - Comparables
    - Days on Market
- Law of Real Estate Agency
    - Customer vs. Client
    - Limited Dual Agency
- Listing agreement
- Get/verify info about property
    - Are you allowed to sell and is there someone who has first right of refusal to buy the property?
    - Square footage
    - Year built
    - Lot size
    - HOA dues, if applicable
    - Unrecorded surveys, easements, or liens.
    - Utilities and average costs
    - Current mortgage amount owed
    - Transferable warranties
    - Property Condition Report

- Lead-based Paint Disclosure
- Security system owned or leased?
- Anything else leased?
- Sellers' goals
  - Why are you selling?
  - How soon do you need to sell?
- Marketing plan
- Advise about prepping property for sale
- Power and water turned on?
- Pre-inspection
  - Sewer/septic
  - well
- Repairs and upgrades
  - Licensed contractor/tradespeople
  - Copy of all work orders and receipts
  - Home warranty
- Landscaping
- Cleaning & decluttering
- Staging

Sales process
- Buyer pre-screening
- Showing instructions/ShowingTime
- What does a good offer look like?
- Earnest Money
- Closing Date
- Buyer financing options
- Waiving contingencies
- Rent-backs
- Appraisal process
- Order title
- Implement repair, landscaping, cleaning, and staging options
- Photograph the property

- Order sign
- Install keybox
- Enter info into MLS
- Prepare other marketing options
- Doorbell neighborhood
- Mail postcards
- Other advertising
- Track all showing activity
- Handle all showing calls and questions ASAP
- Call showing agents for feedback
- Update MLS as needed
- Review market data regularly
- Update sellers weekly or as needed

Receiving offers
- Review ALL offers
- Price
- Earnest Money
- Closing Date
- Financing type and contingency
  - Pre-approval letters
  - Closing costs paid by seller
  - Call lender
- Inspection contingency
- Title contingency
- Buyer positioning statement
- Review net proceeds
- Negotiate offers to mutual acceptance
- Have seller tentatively schedule movers
- Change status to Pending in MLS
- Send contract to title company & lender
- Verify earnest money sent (usually wired or cashier's check dropped at title company)

- Coordinate inspection with buyers' agent, if applicable
- Coordinate appraisal appointment with appraiser
- Review repair requests from inspection report and reply to buyers' agent
- Hire licensed contractor/repairman to take care of all repairs
- Verify repairs have been made to buyers' satisfaction
- Verify title company has all necessary documents, and any issues have been cleared up
- Review final proceeds amounts, loan payoffs, taxes, etc.
- Schedule signing of closing documents and review loan payoff/wiring instructions with escrow
- Submit Powers of Attorney, if applicable
- Mobile notary
- Schedule cancelling/transfer of all utilities
- Coordinate final walk-through with buyers
- Resolve any last-minute issues
- Schedule sign removal
- Provide buyers with home warranty, any transferrable warranty info, keys, garage door openers, etc.
- Change status in MLS to sold

BUYING PROCESS

Pre-Home Search
- Law of Real Estate Agency
  - Customer vs. Client
  - Limited Dual Agency
- Buyer Agency Agreement
- Buyers' goals
- Home buyer checklist/wants & needs
- Current market conditions
  - Multiple offers
  - Interest rates and the cost of waiting
- No home is perfect
  - Inspections—what should and shouldn't be asked for
  - Lead paint
  - Asbestos
  - Radon
- Local info, including schools
- Review financial aspect
  - Financing options
  - Closing Costs
  - Earnest Money
  - Loan process
  - Pre-qualified vs. pre-approved

Searching
- Set up MLS Search
- Pre-screen homes
- Tour properties
- Take notes on all showings
  - Location
  - Amenities
  - Pros and cons

- Days on Market
- Property condition
- Review info on homes of interest
  - Comparables
  - Tax info
  - Schools
    - HOA
    - Easements and zoning
- Review market data weekly

Making offers & getting under contract
- Offer strategies
  - Financing
  - Earnest Money
  - Waiving contingencies
- Inspections
- Home warranty
- Appliance warranties
- Title
- Financing
  - Quick closing
  - Rent-back to sellers
- Negotiate to mutual
- Escrow
- Send contract to title company and lender
- Have buyers tentatively schedule moving company
- Schedule inspection, if necessary
- Schedule appraisal (lender will do this with sellers' agent)
- Deliver earnest money
- Review Title and HOA documents, if not done already
- Attend and review inspection

- Negotiate repairs and/or concessions from inspection
- Re-inspect any repairs
- Keep in regular contact with lender and title company
- Verify buyers' homeowners' insurance
- Schedule and conduct final walk-through
- Ask for average utilities, utility costs, and transferrable warranty documents
- Remind buyers to call all utility companies for hook up
- Have buyers verify with moving company
- Verify funds needed to close/loan paperwork
- Attend closing
  - Wire funds
- Get keys, garage door opener, transferable warranty documents, etc. from seller
- Ensure title company has recorded everything appropriately with the county
- Remind buyers to apply for homestead exemption.

TESTIMONIALS

We have nothing but praise regarding our realtor, Mark Griswold! My husband and I were interested in relocating to an area closer to our daughter. We were unfamiliar with where to look. We did know that we wanted to downsize from a 2 story, 3/4-acre home to a smaller rambler. Mark Griswold was very professional, personable, and knowledgeable. Once he knew our parameters, he diligently researched homes within our requirements. Communication was frequent and he never hesitated on taking us to many listings of homes for sale until we found one to our satisfaction. He was supportive of us for several months after our home closed but before we could move in. You will not get better service than with Mark Griswold of Best Choice Realty/Refuge Properties!
– Robert & Natalie, Rathdrum

Mark is spectacular. Ethical, informed, and hard working on our behalf. Everything you hope you have in a realtor. I give my highest recommendation.
– Carl & Michelle, Ellensburg

I had a great experience working with Mark. I would recommend him to anyone who is looking for a home!
– Russell, Spokane Valley

We called Mark off of a listing when we first came out here in June 2022. We looked at several houses because we kept having needs that were changing. Four trips up here later we finally found the place we liked. The experience was excellent. Zero issues. Mark was always responsive, answering all the questions. Everyone should wish for a Realtor like Mark.
– Max & Angela, Spokane Valley

He was quick, efficient and extremely knowledgeable. The most important part of Mark's sales approach is he never pressured us. Took us to some questionable homes I wanted to see. Guided us when he saw a potential issue...aka the cat house! He knows which one that is. We really enjoyed working with Mark and found him the perfect realtor for us.
                    – Merlon & Mary Ellen, Post Falls

Great help in finding the home we love and getting the price we needed! Mark listens to know what you are looking for and works hard to help you find it!
                    – Kevin & Sherry, Post Falls

We originally planned to start our search for the right home in Northern Idaho proceeding down south and working our way east. However, upon meeting Mark at a home we were interested in, we learned that he and his family had recently moved here and that we shared common values. We formed a great relationship with Mark, and based on our feedback, he took us to a variety of homes over a three-day span until we found the perfect place to call our own. Mark was instrumental in making Northern Idaho our home. Finally, it has been eighteen months since we've purchased our home in Post Falls, and we are more than happy!
                    – James & Pam, Post Falls

Mark Griswold is truly the best real estate agent ever. We have already recommended him to our friends. At our first showing Mark gave us a copy of a book he wrote, The Incomplete Guide to Buying and Selling Your Home, *which proved quite helpful during the entire process. I highly recommend it, along with his services. Mark's customer service is impeccable. He really is there to help make the process easier. Mark showed us so many homes! Every time we called or texted to see a home, he would schedule a viewing for the very next day and often times seeing five or more a day! Each time we viewed a home, if we had any questions Mark couldn't answer, he would text or call the listing agent and have an answer for us before we left the premises. This was so helpful and sealed our commitment to working with him. Upon finding the home we wanted, Mark took the time to call and schedule several vendors for pricing on services needed. We had quotes from vendors in just a couple of days! This was above and beyond anything we expected. This service he provided certainly helped us to make a quicker decision about the purchase and expedited the work needed after our move. Mark always treated us as though we were his most important client. I think that's because Mark really does believe all his clients are his most important client. Thank you Mark for helping us find our new home. We really appreciated everything you did on our behalf. Thank you for introducing us to your sweet family. We are looking forward to our new found friendship. God bless.*

– Mary & John, Post Falls

I honestly can't imagine a better agent to represent me during this purchase. Mark has invested so much time and effort to make sure the transaction went smoothly along with helping me arrange and set up appliances in the house as delivery services messed up my orders. Mark is amazing and super responsive to his clients. Thank you, Mark, for everything you did and continue doing on my behalf.

– Yana, Coeur d'Alene

Mark was great! Very responsive and helpful. He never once complained about our wanting to see a ton of houses in a day. We had complicated loan issues and Mark worked with us and our lender to make the process as easy as possible. Highly recommend!

– Jeff & Glorie, Post Falls